Michael Catt has a remarkable ability to put into words profound truths in simple terms. He has done it again in *The Power of Purpose*. These pages will drive you to your knees before the Savior and compel you to look again at your relationship with Him and the reason He has placed you on this earth. Drawing from the book of Philippians, he has captured the key focus of that great epistle. It is the unbounding, irresistible, and exuberant joy that is found in our purpose in life, which is to know our Lord and become like Him. You will be captivated by these pages . . . and drawn into a fresh relationship with the One who gives us our purpose in life!

James T. Draper Jr.
President Emeritus, LifeWay Christian Resources

This is Michael Catt's best work thus far. Michael, the one known to always ask the pointed questions to make comfortable Christianity uncomfortable, uses the context of the book of Philippians to ask, "If someone was part of your city or church ten years ago and they moved back, would they say you were still on track, living a purposeful life?" Certainly, authentic faith has consistency but it also has conviction. Michael's insights on purposefulness are insightful to those who understand that the gospel is offensive to this world's perspective and Lordship is confrontational to those who bow before the altar of man-pleasing instead of surrendering at the foot of the cross.

John Yeats
Executive Director, Missouri Baptist Convention
Southern Baptist Convention Recording Secretary

I believe Michael Catt to be one of the most gifted expositors of God's Word in the evangelical world today. His sermons and teachings are always biblically grounded, theologically astute, and devotionally enriching; I am encouraged and challenged every time I submit myself to Michael's instruction. In his typical fashion, Michael again delivers faithful, biblical teaching in *The Power of Purpose*. Among the numerous biblical passages that he could have chosen for his study, his selection of the book of Philippians is insightfully appropriate. Michael's exposition of the epistle is guided by his stated conviction: "Purpose matters. But it's not just about having a purpose; it's about having the right purpose." With the heart of a pastor, Michael leads us on a journey through this epistle to teach us what God's 'right purpose' is for individuals and churches.

Having served as a pastor, a professor, and an administrator of Christian universities for over thirty years, I have daily witnessed God's people wrestle to discern His purpose for their lives. Michael Catt has provided an invaluable resource to instruct us on this quest. I enthusiastically commend this work to guide you in this exploration. Knowing God's purpose for your life is a liberating, empowering reality, for as Michael rightfully states, "We were born for purpose. God has gifted you, called you, and empowered you to live a purposeful life." Read this book, learn from Michael's teachings, and embrace the empowering purpose God has for you!

Stan Norman, Ph.D.
Provost and Executive Vice President for Campus Life
Professor of Theology, Oklahoma Baptist University

In a day filled with fear, hopelessness, insecurity, insignificance, immorality, oppression and depression, Dr. Michael Catt's book is a breath of fresh air and a much needed rhema word for this season! IT'S A MUST READ FOR ALL KINGDOM CITIZENS that will educate, equip, enlighten, encourage and enrich!

With historical and biblical exegetical insight, life experience and wisdom, Dr Catt examines the book of Philippians, which is often called the epistle of joy or the believer's mental health book!! He challenges us to break thru with intentional living or living life according to our unique purpose as ordered by the divine Orderer (Ps. 139:14–15; Jer. 1:5)!

We are called according to His purpose, which is to glorify, exalt, and magnify Him that will push back darkness and draw people to the light (Matt. 5:16; Rom. 8:28; 1 Cor. 10:31; Rev. 4:11)!

It is my prayer that this book will help heal hurts and bind up wounds underneath the skin in the unseen realities of life for sinner and saint alike (Ps. 147:3; Luke 4:18)!

I am greatly blessed by Dr. Catt's commitment displayed all over the world, to passionate prayer, enthusiastic evangelism, and great commandment living (Matt. 22:37–40)!! I am praying that God would use this book to stimulate us to model unconditional love, holiness, humility, and brokenness with radical obedience to the Lordship of Jesus Christ that will bring inexplicable unity in the body of Christ ushering in revival in the Church and a Spiritual Awakening in the land!

Thank you my brother, for this excellent work!! May the Savior be glorified, the Saints edified, Satan horrified, and heaven magnified by it!!

K. Marshall Williams Sr.
Senior Pastor, Nazarene Baptist Church, Philadelphia, PA

In what may be his best book yet, Dr. Catt explores a topic that is relevant for everyone but, unfortunately, is lived by few. *The Power of Purpose* is not for the passive. This book is an active call to rise up to the standard of your divine design and live in the rarified air of purposeful intent. Your guide on this journey is a man who has lived out these principles and has seen God do the miraculous time and time again. Get prayed up, get ready to be pressed out, and prepare to live out the power of purpose.

Tally Wilgis
Founding Pastor, Captivate Christian Church
Executive Director, Baltimore Baptist Association

A life without purpose is a meaningless walk in the darkness. The most fully alive people on the planet are those who have discovered that life really does possess meaning and have found their purpose for living. Michael Catt knows something about purpose. As one of America's top communicators he understands how to connect ordinary people with transformative truth. In his new book he skillfully unveils the keys to finding a life of purpose through this skillful exposition of the book of Philippians. Whether you're an individual wanting to take a fresh look at this ancient book or a study group looking for an excellent resource, this book will help you see Philippians in a new way and help you find real life through real purpose.

William Rice
Senior Pastor, Calvary Baptist Church | Clearwater, FL

Michael Catt's book *The Power of Purpose* comes at a time of great spiritual need in North America, and it is desperately needed by today's church. If we're going to reach the millions of lost people across our continent with the gospel, we need God to raise up a new generation of men and women who understand God's purpose for their lives and commit to live it out with everything they have. Read this book and get another copy for a friend. I pray God will use it to ignite a revival of purpose across our continent.

Kevin Ezell
President of the North American Mission Board

THE POWER OF PURPOSE

THE POWER OF PURPOSE

BREAKING THROUGH TO INTENTIONAL LIVING

MICHAEL CATT

B&H
PUBLISHING GROUP

NASHVILLE, TENNESSEE

978-1-4336-5043-7
B&H Publishing Group
Nashville, Tennessee
www.BHPublishingGroup.com

Dewey Decimal Classification: 248.84
Subject Heading: BIBLE. N.T. PHILIPPIANS \ CHURCH \
CHRISTIAN LIFE

Unless otherwise noted, all Scriptures are taken from the
New American Standard Bible (NASB) Copyright © 1960,
1962, 1963, 1968, 1971, 1972, 1973, 1975, 1977, 1995 by The
Lockman Foundation. Used by permission. Other transla-
tions used include: Holman Christian Standard Bible (HCSB),
copyright © 1999, 2000, 2002, 2003, 2009 by Holman Bible
Publishers, Nashville Tennessee. All rights reserved. New
International Version®, NIV® Copyright ©1973, 1978, 1984,
2011 by Biblica, Inc.® Used by permission. All rights reserved
worldwide. New English Translation (NET), NET Bible®
copyright ©1996-2006 by Biblical Studies Press, L.L.C. http://
netbible.com All rights reserved. J.B. Phillips New Testament
(PHILLIPS), The New Testament in Modern English by J.B
Phillips copyright © 1960, 1972 J. B. Phillips. Administered
by The Archbishops' Council of the Church of England. Used
by Permission. The Message (MSG) Copyright © 1993, 1994,
1995, 1996, 2000, 2001, 2002. Used by permission of NavPress
Publishing Group.

Quotations at the beginning of each chapter and other
uncited quotes are taken from John Blanchard's *The Complete
Gathered Gold* (Webster, NY: Evangelical Press, 2006).

Printed in the United States
1 2 3 4 5 6 7   21 20 19 18 17

Dedicated to Andy Andrews

Andy has helped countless numbers of people find their purpose through his writing and speaking. From a young man who was once homeless to now a *New York Times* best-selling author and popular speaker, he asked the question that would bring focus to his life: *Is life just a lottery ticket, or are there choices one can make to direct his future?*

Andy has made deliberate choices in light of who he is in Christ, and he makes me want to be better. His books, stories, emails, and phone calls (always filled with the message of faith, hope, joy, and perseverance) resonate in my heart. My friend has found his purpose and lives it daily, and his focus and determination remind me to pursue mine with the same passion.

CONTENTS

INTRODUCTION: DEFINING OUR PURPOSE

God made us for himself; that is the first and
last thing that can be said about human existence, and whatever more we add is but
commentary.
—A. W. Tozer

SOMEONE HAS SAID that the two greatest days in a person's life are the day he was born and the day he finds out why. Let me start there. I'm adopted. I first learned about my adoption when I was in my late thirties, and to this day I don't know who my birth parents are. But I do know my purpose—I have meaning in life, and I know why I'm here.

A very familiar Scripture on purpose is found in the book of Jeremiah, when the prophet writes, "'For I know the plans that I have for you,' declares the LORD, 'plans for welfare and not for calamity to give you a future and a hope'" (29:11). These words were written some time after the Jews were deported to Babylon around 597 BC to encourage the exiles. Can you imagine how purposeless they felt? God's people had been defeated and exiled. They were probably asking, "What's the use?"

Jeremiah wrote to encourage them, strengthen them, and give them a sense of purpose. Even though they were in captivity, all was not lost. Although they were living in a pagan culture, God had plans for them. It was important for them to be God's witnesses in a pagan world. They needed to follow the one true God while living in Babylon.

DON'T GIVE UP HOPE

Maybe you too have given up hope. Stop thinking that way. As long as God is on the throne, there is hope. None of us knows what may be in store in the days ahead, but we can live with hope. These exiles had lost everything except a few possessions they carried into Babylon. From their perspective, there wasn't much worth living for. If you are a walking pity party, you'll lose your sense of purpose. Whining and complaining won't change a thing. Whether you see your situation as temporary or permanent, if you lose hope, you lose your reason for living. Whatever you are facing, look it in the face and look God in the face and ask Him what He wants you to learn. Wherever you are, it's not an accident. God can take a setback and turn it into a stepping stone.

There is danger if you lack purpose. You start listening to people who tell you what you want to hear. You'll buy lies that make you feel better and feed off spiritual junk food rather than the meat of the Word of God. This was happening with the Babylonian captives. They were listening to false prophets who told them this was a temporary setback that would be over soon. Jeremiah told them the truth. The Scriptures were clear that the Babylonian captivity would be seventy years. Therefore, they needed to settle down, build homes, and get on with their lives. Warren Wiersbe writes, "This small Jewish remnant was holding in its hands the future of God's great plan of salvation, and they must obey Him, be fruitful, and multiply."[1]

HOPE AND PURPOSE

I believe hope and purpose are tied together. If I have a sense of purpose, I have hope. If I have hope, I have a sense of purpose. I find both hope and purpose in the Word of God. Israel was in captivity, yet they needed to be reminded of their purpose. Paul was in prison when he wrote the letter to the Philippians, but he never forgot his purpose. The church is in a battle. We need to remember our purpose. We have a message of hope for a lost world.

As I travel this land, I see people who look empty. They crowd onto subways, planes, and trains, and their faces reveal a lack of purpose. Some look bored. Others seem dazed and confused. For the most part, mankind seems to move through life like cattle headed for the slaughter pen. In the youngest generation—those who should be the most idealistic—there is a sense of dread. They realize they won't have the things their parents had. They graduate from college, can't find a job, and move back home. Social media create a false sense of connection, yet they can't carry on a face-to-face conversation about the real meaning of life. They look empty.

Some people live for their careers. Others focus on finding fulfillment through a soul mate. Many parents allow their lives to be dictated by soccer, ballet, and a thousand other activities that place their children at the center of the universe. Others still focus on fitness, obsessing over exercise, marathons, the gym, or the latest dieting fad. But none of these or the whole host of other false security nets can provide true purpose or lasting satisfaction.

WHAT IS YOUR PURPOSE?

Purpose matters. But it's not just about having a purpose; it's about having the right purpose. Our world is off track. We've lost our way. Everything that used to be wrong is now right. Suicide rates are alarming. Counseling centers can't handle the requests from people whose lives are unraveling. Domestic violence and sexual abuse are ruining the lives of people around the globe. Many seem to have lost (or never truly found) their reason for living. The reality is, we can't live without meaning and purpose. Thomas Carlyle said, "The man without purpose is like a ship without a rudder."[2]

I find great truth in the words of George Eliot: "What makes life dreary is absence of motive. What makes life complicated is multiplicity of motive. What makes life victorious is singleness of motive."[3] Job asked the question, "What is man that You magnify him, and that You are concerned about him, that You examine him every morning and try him at every moment?" (7:17–18). The psalmist asked, "O LORD, what is man, that You take knowledge of him? Or the son of man, that You think of him? Man is like a mere breath; His days are like a passing shadow" (144:3–4). From the Garden to Glory, God has a purpose for man. Life is about discovering that purpose. Fallen man will never find his true purpose until he finds forgiveness and life in Christ. As the early church leader Augustine of Hippo said, "You have made us for yourself, and our hearts are restless, until they can find rest in you." The believer can have Christ and still miss his or her purpose. If we aren't surrendered to the lordship of Christ and walking in the Spirit, we can end up like the children of Israel, wandering in the wilderness of lost opportunity.

The very idea of purpose could not arise by chance, for purpose and chance are opposites. God didn't place us here and wish us good luck. He didn't make us in His image to be a victim of circumstances. He put us here to be overcomers. His witnesses. Salt and light. If it weren't for Jesus, everything in this world would be meaningless. All of life would be a dead-end street. Francis Schaeffer wrote, "Man, made in the image of God, has a purpose: to be in relationship to God, who is there. Man forgets his purpose and thus he forgets who he is and what life means."[4] So let me ask you: What is your purpose?

CHAPTER 1

LIVING A PURPOSEFUL LIFE

Philippians 1:1–2

God doesn't call people who are qualified. He calls people who are willing, and then He qualifies them.
—Richard Parker

I HAVE HUNDREDS of biographies in my personal library—biblical heroes, historical personalities, politicians, entertainers, and sports figures. When you read a biography, you learn things about a person you may have never known by just hearing a few facts about them. Paul often includes biographical snippets in his letters to help us know what's going on in his life. At the beginning of the book of Philippians, he gives readers a glimpse of his own perspective of the current situation: "Paul and Timothy, bond-servants of Christ Jesus, to all the saints in Christ Jesus who are in Philippi, including the overseers and deacons: Grace to you and peace from God our Father and the Lord Jesus Christ" (1:1–2). From these two verses we know who is accompanying Paul and who his audience is.

From a prison cell, the apostle puts pen to parchment with a purpose in mind—to encourage a church that has brought him great joy. This body of believers in Philippi had taken seriously their partnership with Christ. Paul is not thinking about a building, but a people who had made a lasting impression on him.

NO MORE BUSINESS AS USUAL

I've chosen Paul's letter to the Philippians as the focus for this book about purpose. These men and women were assembled in the middle of a corrupt, sensual society, fighting against the trends of political correctness and "business as usual." They were God's representatives in a secular society, and they maintained a singular focus, vision, and purpose.

In the Sacra Script Field Notes on Philippians, the authors note, "Christians who cease to stand out begin to blend into their surrounding culture. When the mind-set and values of secular society concerning lifestyles, faith, morality, responsibility, conduct, marriage, sexuality, and truth influence one's mind and take hold of one's heart they inevitably affect one's attitude and behavior. Society begins to influence the life and mission of the church rather than the other way around. . . . Tragically, light gives way to darkness."[1]

In a world that encourages us to just go with the flow, this letter stands as a reminder of our purpose as Christ-followers. We are called to be the church, the bride of Christ, who stands against the whims of the age. The corrupt culture of the twenty-first century is nothing new. This dichotomy between light and darkness, believers and a lost world, has existed since the beginning of time. In the midst of temptations to conform to or retreat from our society, salt cannot afford to lose its saltiness. If we lack a sense of calling and an understanding of purpose, we'll begin to question God, His character, and His Word.

The church cannot fall into the same trap the Israelites of old fell into. They experienced miraculous deliverance from captivity, but they didn't want to pay the price to take the Promised Land. They forgot their purpose as a people and a nation. When life got difficult or uncomfortable, they moaned of returning to Egypt and slowly began to forget the God of their salvation. We must also avoid the path of compromise, as black and white have been smeared into a dingy gray. If we aren't careful, like Israel, we will compromise, erect idols, and forsake the one true God.

Look around at your community. Once great churches now struggle to merely maintain. Baptismal pools are dry and altars are empty. The church is aging, seemingly indifferent to the next generation. Why? We can blame economics, sociological trends, or changing demographics, but in reality, those are empty excuses. The real issue with a dying church is one thing: we've forgotten our purpose. And sadly, we have little desire to fix the problem.

But Paul's letter to the Philippians holds out hope on the wings of joy in Christ. In this letter we discover how joy can sustain us no matter the circumstances. Many commentators have called it the Epistle of Joy. George Mitchell titled his commentary, *Chained and Cheerful*. Stuart Briscoe preached a sermon series called "Happiness Beyond Our Happenings." You get the picture. This is a book that encourages us to live on a higher plane, unmoved by the winds of change around us.

Paul had countless reasons to complain and throw a pity party, but he chose to be joyful. While imprisoned in Rome, he writes a thank-you note for the financial gift the church at Philippi has invested in his ministry. Yet as he writes, he is reminded of his early experiences in this place with these people. It was not all smooth sailing, but it turned out for a greater good and a greater glory. Ron Dunn used to say to me, "Good and evil run on parallel tracks, and they normally arrive about the same time." This was true in Philippi. God had turned the city around and was using them mightily to advance His kingdom.

These believers lived in a strategic location in the Roman Empire—an economic and military hub located in the Roman colony of Macedonia. Philippi was located on a major road in northern Greece and was home to the first church established in Macedonia. Paul deeply loved this body of believers as evidenced in his intimate, personal letter. He thanks God for them, longs to be reunited with them, and gratefully recognizes the importance of their prayers for him. Regardless of his own future, Paul didn't want these fellow saints to lose their focus in the days ahead.

I imagine that countless memories about Philippi flooded Paul's mind as he wrote. He must have thought of Lydia and her Bible study group. He probably reminisced about the demon-possessed girl who had been delivered and remembered how God had opened doors in that strategic city. I'm sure he even reflected on God's saving grace that rescued the jailer who only a few hours before had beaten Paul and Silas and thrown them into prison. A smile possibly graced his face as he thought back on that experience when, beaten and bloody, he and Silas started singing praise songs to God. Through it all, God had done a great work in Philippi, and Paul was encouraged to know it was continuing.

How do you view life? Do you see setbacks as part of God's plan? Is your tendency to moan, groan, and complain, or to rejoice? Would anyone say you have the gratitude attitude? Stuart Briscoe urges, "When you find yourself in prison, or in a hospital bed, or tied to a kitchen sink, or anchored to an office desk, it's a good thing to remember what God has been doing in your life instead of moaning about your present status."[2]

Not every church is known for being the kind of church that someone like Paul would be proud to be a part of. What is your church known for? What is your city known for? If someone was a part of your city and church ten years ago and they came back or wrote a letter to you, would they be able to say that you were still on track, living a purposeful life?

Unfortunately, many churches are known for what they used to be. Once great buildings are now abandoned or deteriorating. Why? They lost their sense of purpose and calling. Whether we like it or not, America is by and large a post-Christian nation. We've lost our purpose as a nation because we've lost our purpose as the people of God. One reason our great cities are filled with crime and hatred is because churches abandoned our cities and moved to the suburbs decades ago, and we are now living with the consequences of a lost purpose, vision, and passion for things that matter.

Many cities fail to change with the times and lose their purpose in the process. I visited a city in New England a few years ago that once was the largest carriage and coach center in America. But when the automobile emerged, they didn't adjust to the times, and the times passed them by—and now that town is just another spot along the road.

Cities are often known for some distinguishing site, industry, or historical figure. Jerusalem is known as the City of God and the center of Jewish life. New York is marked by Wall

Street, Broadway, and the Yankees. Atlanta is affiliated with Chick-fil-A and Coca-Cola. Los Angeles is recognized as the hot spot for celebrities and the television and film industries. The city where I live, Albany, Georgia, is the birthplace of Ray Charles, Patti LaBelle, and Ray Stevens, among others. Unfortunately, this "Good Life City" is in decline and has been recognized as the fourth poorest city in America. Most churches are dead or dying, major industries have left, and many lament the problems without offering any solutions. It's a tough place to serve, but it's home for Sherwood Church and my family, and we believe God put us here for a purpose.

PURPOSEFUL CHURCH

All across the world there are churches that stand out when you hear their names—some because of their great impact and others because of what they used to be. The Moody Church in Chicago is still a vibrant, vital force in the city where D. L. Moody started his work. However, the Metropolitan Tabernacle in London, where the great Charles Spurgeon pastored, is a mere shadow of what it was in the nineteenth century. The Church in the Dump in Cairo houses more than ten thousand people who literally meet in a garbage dump each week. Many of the churches in South Korea, and the Brooklyn Tabernacle in New York City, are known for their prayer meetings. The church I pastor is typically known for making movies. Those movies were never our purpose, but they have been a tool in helping us achieve our purpose to touch the world from Albany, Georgia. In 2015, my family and I took a trip to Italy. The cathedrals were beautiful and ornate, but they were mostly empty except for tourists. We even saw small groups of people gathered to worship while hundreds and hundreds of tourists were snapping pictures of statues, frescos, and mosaics. When a place of worship becomes a tourist site, there's been a loss of purpose.

Paul probably would not have mentioned some of the things on our list when we talk about what makes a church great. He measured by standards that wouldn't fit on an annual report. If someone wrote a letter about you or your church, would you be concerned about the content? Would you be fearful of the revealed facts? Overwhelmingly, Philippians is a positive letter. Yes there were concerns, but Paul wrote a great deal about his own life, mission, and purpose, while reminding these believers about theirs.

Since the early 2000s, I've been traveling the country with a team of pastors leading ReFRESH® Conferences. We've served and ministered to thousands of pastors and lay leaders as we seek to call the church back to Christ in revival. We've discovered that many pastors and lay leaders are discouraged and have lost their sense of calling. When that happens, purpose is lost. I've talked to hundreds of pastors who are struggling with ministry, identity, calling, and lack of purpose. Many are close to giving up. Some are hoping the grass will be greener on the other side.

If that's you, if you're in that place of hoping the grass is greener on the other side, let me ask you a question: Why are you breathing? I often ask that when trying to share the gospel with a stranger. It's a purposeful question. It demands thought and some kind of response. So, allow me to apply that question in the context of purpose. What's your purpose in life? Why has God placed you on planet Earth? Is it just to grow up, get married, have kids, get a job, and ultimately retire and die? Surely there's more to life than that. I once saw a gravestone that said, "Born a human being, died a wholesale grocer." We were born for purpose. God has gifted you, called you, and empowered you to live a purposeful life. Don't miss it. If you don't live on purpose, you'll miss a great adventure.

To Nurture, To Love

CHAPTER 2

PURPOSEFUL PRAYER
Philippians 1:1–5

Lack of praying does not handicap us; it paralyzes us.
—Warren Wiersbe

Nothing is so deadening to the divine as an habitual dealing with the outside of holy things.
—George MacDonald

IN ONE WAY or another, every aspect of the Christian life, when lived out properly, has a definite purpose. If we are purposeful, we seek to glorify God, share our faith, study the Scriptures, and take seriously what it means to be a disciple. Interestingly, the only thing Jesus' disciples asked Him to teach them was how to pray (Luke 11:1ff). So if we're serious about being Christ-followers, then we'll also be purposeful about prayer.

However, studies reveal (and if we're honest we would all admit) that prayer is the hardest thing we do as believers. For many it's a desperate plea only in times of crisis; for a few others it's their purpose and calling to intercede for others. But for most of us, prayer lacks purpose, structure, and consistency.

We all love the idea of people praying for us. We post on social media that we are praying when someone shares a serious situation. We casually tell people at church that we'll be praying and then forget it before we even get to our car. But what if prayer was purposeful, intentional, and focused? Samuel Taylor Coleridge wrote, "The act of praying is the very highest energy of which the human mind is capable; praying, that is, with the total concentration of the faculties."[1]

Take a moment and remind yourself that Jesus ever lives to make intercession on your behalf (Heb. 7:25). Jesus is praying for you *right now* in heaven. The Spirit lives in you and is praying for you *right now* (Rom. 8:26). Clearly, one of the purposes of our eternal God is prayer for the saints. Let's not allow our prayers to die while our Intercessor lives.

Purposeful prayer is bold in approaching the throne of grace, and it is specific. General prayers yield general answers; specific prayers yield specific answers. We must move beyond the elementary praying of, "Bless those for whom it is our duty to pray" and "Bless the gift and the giver."

POWERLESS WITHOUT PRAYER

There is a stark reality revealed in the Christian life that believers cannot rise above the level of their personal prayer life. If we want to live on purpose for God, we need a guiding hand. Prayer is the system of checks and balances where we don't just talk to God, but God also speaks to our hearts. Bob Cotton notes, "True prayer is rooted in the promises and covenants of God, in His past achievements, in His ability to do immeasurably more than all we ask or imagine."[2]

If we aren't purposeful in prayer, we are powerless, both individually and corporately. A church is no stronger than her prayer ministry. Given the fact that Paul was constantly on the run, planting churches, evangelizing the lost, and defending the faith against the Judaizers and Gnostics, it's amazing to see the depth of his prayers. The apostle's prayers impacted the world, emboldened the church, and caused the devil to shudder. Might I suggest that one reason our churches are prayerless is because many of our church members aren't members of Christ.

Although there are thousands of books on prayer, we find little prayer in our churches today. According to one survey, the average pastor prays less than five minutes a day. The church prayer meeting has gone the way of the dinosaur. If you want to kill attendance in the average church, call a prayer meeting. George Duncan wrote, "One lesson that stands out vividly in this particular passage is that the *work* of God depends upon the *men* of God and ultimately upon *obedience* to God. . . . The whole issue that God has with the church does not lie in the realm of ignorance—already we *know* so much; it is our obedience that is at fault, we fail to *do* the will of God."[3]

At Sherwood we have purposefully planned for a multifaceted Intercessory Prayer Ministry.

- Our Prayer Tower is available to our members twenty-four hours a day.
- We have prayer altars at the front of the Worship Center.
- As a staff, we pray for ten families each week and write prayer cards to them.
- When we built the current Worship Center, we built a prayer closet under the platform (Spurgeon's Prayer Room) where intercessors gather on Sundays to pray during the services.
- I send out an email to more than four hundred intercessors almost every week with specific prayer requests regarding my ministry and family.
- We have a "House of Prayer" on Sunday evenings prior to the service.
- Each year we fill out HIM-possible cards (needs you have that only God can meet) and lay them on the altar for people to pray over.

Have you ever met someone whose purpose in life was prayer? I have. These people have been used by God to stir, challenge, and convict me. Don Miller was the greatest man of prayer I ever met. He traveled the world for decades teaching prayer conferences, and he knew how to take God at His Word. I have a brief recording of Don in his nineties, praying for me shortly before he died.

I remember sitting at a staff retreat in the '90s and asking, "If you could ask just one person to pray for you, who would it be?" Two of us named Linda Breland. Ask her husband, her children and grandchildren, the young women she disciples, or her friends, and they will affirm that Linda is a prayer warrior. She can spend all day in prayer and often does. She has bombarded heaven on behalf of my family more times than I can count.

Throughout most of my twenty-five-plus years at Sherwood, I have met weekly with a small group of older men in our church who pray for me. I have grieved deeply when a couple of them have passed away, and the void in my life without them is great. One of those men was John Dees. More than a loyal layman, John was a friend, father figure, leader, and prayer warrior. He was a giant of a man in every way. His wife told me there were times when she would get up in the night and hear him in the den, calling out my name before God. At one point, this elderly couple considered moving to another state to be closer to one of their daughters, but John wouldn't even consider it. "Michael needs me," he would say. And I did. I'm grateful that the aroma of his prayers still lingers at the throne of grace.

THE POWER OF PURPOSE

Warren Wiersbe has our family picture sitting on his desk so he can see it as he prays for us each day. I was doing a men's conference for former Southern Baptist Convention President Ronnie Floyd a few years ago. In front of six hundred men, he showed me on his iPad where he prayed for me every day and had been for years—I had no clue. I have a small prayer team of men and women outside the church that I often email or text with specific prayer requests. I can't begin to explain how vital the prayers of the saints are to me. I'm convinced that I would not have made it this far if people hadn't prayed for me along the way. These men and women are the intercessors who stand between porch and altar and plead before the throne in my stead (Joel 2:17). I'm grateful and blessed by every prayer offered to the Father on my behalf. It brings calm assurance during times of uncertainty, hope amid fear, and comfort in the pain.

I wonder what it was like to be on Paul's prayer list. In many of his letters, he takes time to include a prayer for the church. I find it no small thing that the inerrant, inspired, infallible Word of God includes specific prayers. These prayers were not ramblings; they were purposeful and pointed, and they act as a guide for our own praying. If you don't know how to pray, pray Scripture.

PRAYING FOR THE SAINTS

So who is Paul praying for? "Paul and Timothy, bond-servants of Christ Jesus, to all the saints in Christ Jesus who are in Philippi, including the overseers and deacons: Grace to you and peace from God our Father and the Lord Jesus

Christ" (Phil. 1:1–2). He prays for all the saints, and specifically for the leaders.

Make note that the apostle refers to himself and Timothy as bond-servants. Everything about Paul's purpose in life hinged on his understanding of what it meant to be a bond-servant of Jesus Christ. True leaders understand that the key to their success is obedience. I believe you learn obedience when you are alone with God. My friend Roger Breland always reminds us, "God will never use you in public until He tutors you in private." Paul was totally available to God, and that surrendered life was evident in his prayers.

Paul addresses this letter to saints. These precious men and women at Philippi were saints in the eyes of God—God's servants on this earth. Paul viewed them as a body totally available to the Lord Jesus. *Saint* is, in fact, the key term for believers in the New Testament. The word *Christian* is used three times, but some form of the word *saint* is used more than sixty times. When J. B. Phillips wrote his paraphrase of the New Testament, he replaced the word *saints* with *true Christians*. That's not a bad way to interpret the word!

In *Vine's Expository Dictionary*, the word *saint* is defined: "In the plural, as used of believers, it designates all . . . and is not applied merely to persons of exceptional holiness, or to those who having died, were characterized by exceptional acts of 'saintliness.' The church doesn't make you a saint. Christ makes you a saint. We are saints 'in Christ Jesus.'"[4]

When Paul penned the opening words to his first letter to the Corinthians, he wrote "To the church of God which is at Corinth, to those who have been sanctified in Christ Jesus, saints by calling" (1:2). What does that mean? It means the church is a divine possession with a local manifestation. We are saints who are bond-servants. We don't strut; our purpose is to serve to the glory of God.

Paul wants them to understand what they've become in Christ. They are partakers of the divine nature. They are not just saints, but saints "in Christ Jesus." There is no hint of self-effort, self-improvement, or trying harder. And this isn't just a title reserved for those of extraordinary service or performing miracles. It's the DNA of every believer. We've been saved and are being sanctified by Christ. We work and serve, but not to *be* saved; we serve because we *have been* saved. William Booth, founder of the Salvation Army, said, "Work as if everything depended upon work and pray as if everything depended upon prayer."

Paul points out the temporary offices of overseer and deacon, but he groups them in the eternal calling of *saints*. This word is tied to the word *holy* and teaches us that all purposeful people live set-apart lives. They don't have time to be bogged down in the generally insignificant. However, we shouldn't rush past the reference to overseers and deacons. It's a reminder to pray for the spiritual leaders of the church. Are you praying for your pastor? For missionaries on the front lines of spiritual warfare? For the laity who serve children and youth? These leaders are not only worthy of double honor, but they are also worthy of intentional prayer. Intercession on behalf of others should be personal and purposeful.

On the other hand, it's important that we not get caught up in titles. The purpose of life is not to become a church officer or title-holder. If your purpose is a title or an office, you've missed the whole point and you already have your reward. If you insist on being called Doctor, Reverend, Brother So-and-So, the issue may be more with your own insecurities than with someone else's "lack of respect" for the office. Your purpose in life is to know God—settling for anything less will result in disappointment and heartache.

Paul recognized his recipients and then went immediately to prayer. Why did he write down his prayer for the Philippians? I believe it's a reminder to us that prayer is more than lip service. It's one thing to tell someone you're praying for them; it's another to be purposeful in your praying. As one preacher of another era used to say, "Pray 'til you pray!"

FOR WHAT SHOULD WE PRAY?

I'm sure there was a prayer list at the church in Philippi with many significant physical needs. But the apostle rarely asked for prayer in the physical realm, nor did he focus on physical needs in the churches to whom he wrote. I know a person who is always trying to figure out a way to be on everyone's prayer list. They do have health issues, but every now and then there's an insistence to be on the list because they "need encouragement." I'm guessing all the members of our church family need encouragement from time to time.

Paul's primary list probably wouldn't have focused on physical needs; he prayed that the church might not have spiritual casualties. Let's be honest: we are all going to die. But what we are, who we are, and how we live before we get to heaven are of greater importance than our physical needs. In reality, we can't control the physical, but we can be purposeful in praying for spiritual fruit that remains. Alan Redpath wisely said, "Much of our praying is just asking God to bless some folks that are ill, and to keep us plugging along. But prayer is not merely prattle, it is warfare."[5]

Recently, I preached a series on prayer titled, "Next Level Praying." In one of those messages, I shared with our church family how to pray for me and for the church staff. It's important for us to pray for those in authority. Ask God to pour out His Spirit in undeniable ways on the leader and to provide:

- An overwhelming sense of His presence
- A desire for holiness
- Zeal and love for Jesus
- The power of the Holy Spirit
- Clear discernment of God's will
- A safeguard against Satan's influence
- Protection for their marriage and family
- Increasing fruitfulness in ministry
- Pure motives

After identifying the object of his prayers, Paul then writes of the purpose behind his praying: "I thank my God in all my remembrance of you, always offering prayer with joy in my every prayer for you all, in view of your participation in the gospel from the first day until now" (Phil. 1:3–5). Paul was thankful for a church that was intentional about spreading the gospel. He had wonderful memories of this church that spilled over into his prayers of gratitude.

Memory is a powerful thing—either a blessing or a curse. Having served both carnal and unified churches in several states, I can tell you that memories, good or bad, last a lifetime. When I remember the people who have blessed my life, my eyes well up with humble tears and a smile comes to my face. However, when I remember people who resisted the Holy Spirit, divided churches, fell into sin, or compromised their integrity, my heart breaks.

Lehman Strauss writes, "There was no conflict, no confusion, but continuance. A continuing fellowship is a prayer fellowship."[6] It seems wherever Paul went, he had fond memories of the Philippians. He probably told stories about his ministry there and may have used some of those saints as examples in his sermons. Sitting in a Roman prison, Paul had a thankful heart as he sat down to write this short letter. Though some churches had brought him pain, this one brought him great joy and made a marked difference in the apostle's life.

When was the last time you intentionally prayed for or wrote a letter of gratitude to someone who invested in your life? In a text message and Instagram world, handwritten notes are no longer the way we communicate. However, I would submit that no one keeps a text message forever. I have letters that were written to me forty years ago that are still in my files.

During our weekly House of Prayer gatherings, Sherwood members write hundreds of prayer cards that are sent across our community and around the world. Rarely a week goes by that I don't hear someone mention those handwritten cards. I could tell you stories of people who have received so many prayer cards that they've blanketed a wall with them. Others have placed them in baskets beside their bed as a reminder of the prayers of the saints. Who are you praying for by name? What prompts you to pray daily?

George Raindrop, in his book *No Common Task*, tells how a nurse once taught a dull, disgruntled, and dispirited man to pray, and he was transformed into a man of joy. Much of the nurse's work was done with her hands, and each finger served as a prompt for prayer. Her thumb was nearest to the rest of her body, and it reminded her to pray for those who were closest to her heart. The second finger was used for pointing, and it reminded her of all her teachers in school and in the hospital. The third finger was the tallest and reminded the nurse of the V.I.P.s—the leaders in every sphere of life. The fourth finger, the weakest, reminded her of those who were in trouble or pain. Finally, the little finger was the smallest and least important, and, to the nurse, it represented herself.[7]

GRATEFUL AND THANKFUL

As Paul was reminded ("in all my remembrance of you"), he immediately moved to thanksgiving. When memories would come to his mind of the church in Philippi, the overwhelming sense of joy and pride drove him to prayer. And that prayer was focused on thanksgiving. Unfortunately we don't hear "thank you" much anymore. We've indulged our children so much that they are rarely grateful for what they have. A few years ago I asked four or five children if they got what they wanted for Christmas. All of them said, "No!" Clearly we've lost our gratitude attitude.

I believe being grateful and thankful is an intentional choice we must make until it becomes a part of our spiritual DNA. We are children of Adam and Eve, who weren't grateful for the perfect, sinless environment God gave them. And now we too, far removed from Eden yet closely linked in heart to those two, grow ungrateful for the grace and mercy God has given to us.

Why not sit down with a legal pad and just start listing all the things you could and should be grateful for? Start with the ability to write and think. People don't hesitate to call a prayer meeting in a crisis, but we are slow to call a praise meeting when God steps in. A church that doesn't pray can't expect the blessings of God, and a church that fails to thank God and count their blessings will soon take their blessings for granted.

Ingratitude will never attract a lost world. We are to be the aroma of Christ in this decaying culture, yet we've become so inwardly focused that we assume God owes us blessings and answered prayers. We expect people to do things for us. Remember when Jesus healed the ten lepers and only one of them returned to thank Him? I'm afraid most of us would be counted in the nine who kept walking.

The apostle's remembrance led to gratitude, and that gratitude drove him to intercession: "always offering prayer with joy in my every prayer for you all, in view of your participation in the gospel from the first day until now" (1:4–5). John Eadie writes, "The supplicant thanks while he asks and blesses as he petitions."[8] Paul was thankful and full of joy. Interceding for this church energized him. When we petition the throne of grace on behalf of others, we aren't just going through a list of requests; we are asking God to help us enter into others' situations, needs, victories, and failures.

In his intercession, Paul begins to focus on their partnership. The word *participation* in verse 5 is the Greek word *koinonia*, meaning "communion." Partnerships imply we have common ground—a common goal, cause, vision, or purpose. Partners work together for the greater good and understand that more can be done together than alone. The Philippians' participation was gospel-centered; they contended for the faith (1:27). It was personal, as they invested in Paul's ministry and gave of their own resources to support him financially. And it was continual, "from the first day until now" (1:5). This was a long-standing relationship built on intentionality. The Philippians purposed in their hearts to bless Paul, and Paul purposed in his heart to edify them. Therefore we see Paul's joy was fourfold:

1. *The joy of recollection (v. 3)*—I may not experience great joy when I recall some past experiences like my high school days. But I do have joy inexpressible when I remember the way God has faithfully answered prayers, the doors He has opened and closed, and the provision He has made.

2. *The joy of intercession (v. 4)*—Paul's focus on other people and his way of using each remembrance as a prompt to pray should encourage us to strive for the same. When someone randomly crosses your mind, it isn't random at all. Take that name before the Father, and turn that memory into a moment of intercession.

3. *The joy of participation (v. 5)*—Certainly Paul could have strutted in his own accomplishments as the greatest missionary of all time. But he understood that his ministry didn't happen in a vacuum and that he enjoyed (and desperately needed) the cooperation of the saints to do what God had called him to.

4. *The joy of anticipation (v. 6)*—Manley Beasley used to always ask, "What are you believing God for today?" What are you anticipating? If we are going to be purposeful, we must anticipate and move with God.

Pause here and ask who the Lord has brought to your remembrance as you've read and pondered Paul's prayer. This simple BLESS outline from my friend Doug Small has helped me immeasurably in praying a blessing over people's lives as they come to mind.[9]

- **B**ody—Pray for physical things (housing, health, healing, etc.).
- **L**abor—Pray for work needs, job issues, employment concerns.
- **E**motion—Pray for peace of mind, fulfillment, happiness, joy.

- Social—Pray for relationships, marriage, children, family concerns.
- Spiritual—Pray for their salvation or for their maturity in Christ, that they walk in His fullness, in repentance, and in awakening.

If we are going to be purposeful in prayer, we must define what that means. What adjustments need to be made? What have we formerly failed to pray for? Let me make a few suggestions.

Prayer is not optional. It's not an afterthought, either personally or corporately. Prayer should direct our thinking. Prayer isn't merely a bridge between songs in the worship service on Sundays, and it isn't our personal to-do list back to God as if He is running errands for us. The prayerless Christian is a danger to himself and to his church. When our knees are not bent, our feet soon begin to wander.

Our commitment to prayer can't be passive. We must intensify our praying. When God has moved in seasons of refreshing and revival, it is because people have gone to extraordinary levels of praying. They have begun to cry out to God.

John Hull and Tim Elmore write:

> Praying to make a difference . . . is a refreshing engagement of God when compared to the myopic mantras like "God bless me and mine," so often heard these days. American Christian culture, nowadays hypnotized by consumerism and self-interest, is plagued with egocentric

prayer. We might as well say, "God, it's all about me!" because that's where we spend a lot of our prayer time.[10]

God is watching and waiting for intercessors who are intentional. If we want to see God move powerfully in answer to prayer, we can't be flippant about praying. E. M. Bounds said, "Prayer honours God, acknowledges his being, exalts his power, adores his providence, secures his aid."[11]

Revivalist preacher Duncan Campbell remarked, "God, do you not know that your honor is at stake? You promised to pour out water on the thirsty. God, you know you are not doing it. God, I am thirsty! Everyone knows God reigns, my God, I now on the basis of Christ's atonement challenge you to fulfill your covenant engagement with men and do it now!"[12]

We need to be praying for revival in the church and awakening in the land. Revival presupposes life, yet so many of our churches are dead. Awakening is what happens in the world when the church is revived. All across America and Europe the church is in a serious state of apathy and decline. We swap sheep from one fold to another, but we aren't reaching the lost. We've bought the lie that the answer is in more rules, legalism politics, education reform, isolation from the world . . . and the list goes on and on. Paul would say we've missed the point. While living in a depraved, pagan culture, he understood that the power to change the Roman Empire was not in electing a new Caesar, but in surrendering to the lordship of Christ and allowing His life to be lived through broken vessels in a dark and decaying world.

We can't change the course or stem the tide of decline, cynicism, anger, bitterness, hurt, and distrust by sheer willpower or through legislation. The times demand a spiritual remedy. The one common denominator in every historic move of God has been prayer. At some point we are going to leave the church to the next generation. The question is: What kind of church will we leave?

Stop worrying. Stop fretting. Start praying. Oswald Chambers wrote, "Worry is an indication that we think God cannot look after us."[13] Vance Havner noted, "It is not work but worry that kills, and it is amazing how much wear the human mind and body can stand if it is free from friction and well-oiled by the Spirit."[14] We can't worry and pray at the same time—the two are completely incompatible.

Prayer is a key component to making disciples. Jesus spent the night in prayer before He called His disciples. The disciples asked, "Lord, teach us to pray" (Luke 11:1). We need to be intentional in teaching new believers that the Christian life is a life of dependence on God. Any mentoring, leadership, or discipleship in the church that doesn't include prayer will fizzle out in fleshly efforts.

Prayer is not the foundation or the groundwork before the work; it *is* the work. We shouldn't start something and then tack on a prayer and ask God to bless it. Our work for the kingdom must begin, continue, and end in prayer. If we are going to work for God, we must pray for the power we need to do the work.

In 1650, Jeremy Taylor wrote these words about prayer:

> Christ has put [the power of prayer] into the hands of men, and the prayers of men have saved cities and kingdoms from ruin; prayer has raised dead men to life, has stopped the violence of fire, shut the mouths of wild beasts, altered the course of nature, caused rain in Egypt and drought in the sea. Prayer rules over all gods; it arrests the sun in its course and stays the chariot wheels of the moon; it reconciles our suffering and weak faculties with the violence of torment and the violence of persecution; it pleases God and supplies all our need.[15]

PRAYER AND EVANGELISM

Prayer and evangelism are inseparable. We will pray for lost people by name, and we will pray for the saved to grow in maturity and go into the fields to win the lost. A few years ago I was preaching at a Methodist church growth conference, and the pastor told me about a bishop in South America. People come to this man and say, "I want to start a church." So he asks, "How many people did you lead to Christ this week?" "None." "How many did you lead to Christ last week? Last month? In the last six months?" "None." "Okay. You go start winning people to Jesus and come see me in a year and we'll talk about it."

"The unsaved person doesn't understand the Christian; they live in two different worlds. But the Christian understands the unsaved person."[16] "The prayer in Jesus' name drives the enemy off the battlefield of man's will and leaves him free to choose right."[17] "Evangelism is merely going out into the fields white unto harvest and picking up the spoils of victory won by prayer."[18]

Over the past couple of years the term *extraordinary prayer* has been used often among those who long to see God move in a new and fresh way in our land. It's an old revival term that implies crying out to God. As my friend Bill Elliff told me, "Whatever extra-ordinary prayer is, it's more than what we are doing now." When you read the Scriptures and study the history of revival, the prayer warriors became very purposeful. They cried out to God to move, rend the heavens, heal the land, forgive sin, restore, and return.

In a sermon during one of our ReFRESH® Conferences, Bill illustrated this thought of intense, watchful praying in an unforgettable way. He talked about the difference in normal praying and crying out to God in desperation. "What would be different about your prayer life if you were asking God to bless your daughter who just graduated from college, got a new job, moved into her own apartment, and was walking with the Lord versus interceding for your daughter who had been kidnaped and was missing in a foreign country?" One prayer would be general, the other very desperately specific. In the first situation we would typically mumble half-heartedly through the prayer.

In the other we would be on our knees, begging God to hear our cries.

At the beginning of this chapter, I mentioned some men and women who've had a profound impact on my life in the area of prayer—one of those was Don Miller. Don was the most purposeful prayer warrior I've ever known, and when I think of purposeful praying, he's the first person who comes to mind. His son Gary recounts his father's encounter with Christ that changed the course of his life forever:

> The day Dad was saved, God called him to preach. He met Christ after attending a worship service at First Baptist Church in Monroe, Louisiana. He returned to his post at Selmon Field near Swartz, Louisiana. As he sat on the steps of a tarpaper-shacked barrack, a young soldier from Alabama sat down next to him. They discussed what they had heard that morning and had to admit that, if what that preacher said was true, they were lost. They didn't know what else to do but to shake hands and agree to receive Jesus as their Savior. Dad never saw the young soldier again, but he never stopped walking hand in hand with Jesus. I can never remember when prayer was not a priority in Dad's life. It was impossible to get up earlier than him. He raced to Jesus before the light rose in the sky.

Still, there came a dark day in December 1975 when Dad was near death and facing another serious surgery at Baylor Hospital in Dallas. In January of that year, he had selected his verse for 1975: "That I may know Him and the power of His resurrection and the fellowship of His suffering" (Philippians 3:10). During that year, Dad's colon burst and he faced three life-threatening surgeries. He contracted peritonitis and wore three colostomies on his body to remove the infection. As a result, Dad was unable to preach for a year. During a long, dark night in ICU he heard God's Spirit confirm to him that he would preach again, but his calling would be to the ministry of prayer. The verse God gave him was Psalm 18:28, "For thou wilt light my candle: the Lord my God will enlighten my darkness."

Dad returned to his home church, North Shore Baptist in Long Island, and preached for a year. Then he moved to Fort Worth in June 1977 to begin Bible Based Ministries and actively conducted prayer conferences around the world until 2010. He and Mom conducted over a thousand conferences in forty-nine states and on five continents.

As far as Dad's sole purpose, his own words from his hospice bed prior to his death say it best:

"God and I are intertwined like two fingers crossed, waiting for whatever God has for me in Jesus. I am waiting on His schedule. Romans 8:28 comes to mind. Prayer has always been the solid platform to stand on when everything else is shaking. I am still amazed that God let a fellow like me be in on it. I moved from the pastoral role to the prayer role. It has always been the main thing. I focus on an Audience of One now."

CHAPTER 3

A PURPOSEFUL PERSPECTIVE

Philippians 1:6–21

Every church Paul founded was an answer to prayer, every letter Paul wrote was born from a heart of prayer, every sermon Paul preached was bathed in the power of prayer. Paul prayed sensibly, specifically, sensitively and supernaturally.

—Sam Gordon

I AM FASCINATED with the life of C. S. Lewis—his brilliant mind, conversion to Christ, ability to defend the faith, and profound writings. In many ways, Lewis and the apostle Paul are much alike. Both men experienced a radical transformation that led to a powerful position of influence.

A number of years ago the movie *Shadowlands*, starring Anthony Hopkins as C. S. Lewis, was released worldwide. In the film, Lewis returns to Oxford from London. He had married Joy Gresham, an American woman, in a private Episcopal ceremony performed at her hospital bedside. She was dying from cancer, and a relationship that began with letters back and forth had blossomed into deep love. When Lewis arrives at Oxford he is met by Harry Harrington, an Episcopal priest, who asks what news there is. Lewis hesitates, then, deciding to speak of the marriage and not the cancer, he says, "Ah, good news, I think, Harry. Yes, good news."

Harrington, not aware of the marriage and thinking that Lewis is referring to Joy's medical situation, replies, "I know how hard you've been praying. . . . Now, God is answering your prayer." "That's not why I pray, Harry," Lewis responds. "I pray because I can't help myself. I pray because I'm helpless. I pray because the need flows out of me all the time, waking and sleeping. It doesn't change God; it changes me."[1]

Paul, as we have already seen, was a man of prayer. It would be a temptation to rush past Paul's prayer and get to the good stuff. But this is the good stuff. What we can learn from Paul will help us. If we don't gain a purposeful perspective through prayer, we will waste our lives in secondary activities that have little if any eternal value.

God's plan is for us to be like Jesus. Don Miller said in a sermon, "Prayer is the intimate communication between the heavenly Father and His child." Out of Paul's intimacy with the Father came instructions. He had something to say, but it wasn't his fleshly opinion. It was the Word of God communicated to Paul in his prayer closet.

It's easier to preach or write about prayer than to pray. All of us could admit that we talk more about prayer than we pray. Gary Miller said, "Effective prayer is not about practiced elocution or posturing eloquence. It is about the profound exasperation of the warrior in the middle of desperate circumstances and in the face of a relentless enemy."[2]

As Paul writes, he does so from the assumption that these people are all in. There were no first and third Sunday, Easter and Christmas church members here. These were believers who surrendered to Christ in every area of their lives. And remember, Paul is not writing from a condo on the beach; he's in prison. He has been beaten, attacked, accused, and forsaken by many, but these folks stood with him. When the going got tough, they didn't bail out on him. Love builds love. They loved Paul, and Paul loved them.

In the early 2000s, the best Bible conference teacher and one of my dearest friends went to be with the Lord. He taught his last conference at the church where he had his greatest ministry, MacArthur Boulevard in Irving, Texas. Ron Dunn was known across America and around the world as a great expositor and man of prayer. MacArthur Boulevard lived in perpetual revival for a number of years under Ron's leadership as he led the church to start an Intercessory Prayer Ministry. In that season of revival, he confronted the handful of troublemakers and said that their divisive spirit was going to stop. It did.

When Ron preached that final conference, he was weak and frail after months of being in and out of hospitals. When he stood to preach, he said that the past few months had reminded him of what matters most in life. I want to take his main sermon points and weave my thoughts together with his into this part of the chapter. They helped me, and I believe they will help you too.

You can't read Paul's letter without thinking of words like *joy, rejoicing,* and *thanksgiving.* We tend to thank God only when things are going our way. In the Bible, thanksgiving is related to spiritual blessings—those things that time, circumstance, persecution, or adversity cannot take away. Thanksgiving is a matter of perspective. Any of us could look at life and play the "poor, poor pitiful me" game. As Ron was struggling physically, he was deepening spiritually. He came up with a list of things he was thankful for. I would call this a list with a purposeful perspective.

OUR FRIENDS IN THE FAITH

As Paul reminisced, he had no regrets about his days in Philippi—even the time spent in jail. No one lives the Christian life in isolation. From a biblical perspective, the church is to be a family from every tribe and tongue. We come from various cultures, backgrounds, and influences, but we have found a common purpose in Christ.

I've pastored Sherwood Church in Albany since the late 1980s. It's certainly not the easiest city to live in, where crime, gangs, divorce, drugs, and poverty are rampant. In recent years we were named the fourth poorest city in America. But in the midst of this darkness, God has made Himself clearly visible in multiple ways. We have people from twenty nations and various cultural influences who meet together because of the common bond of Christ.

If relationships aren't supernatural, they are superficial. I have friends closer than brothers. I consider the church body to be my family. God hasn't always given me what I wanted, but He has given me so much more: an incredible wife, two daughters, a church family, and other ministers and friends who are dear to me. I am a blessed man because of friends in the faith. We should all remember there are no lone rangers in the Christian life. Even the Lone Ranger had Tonto.

OUR FELLOWSHIP IN THE GOSPEL

Paul and the church in Philippi were partners with a common purpose. We need each other, and we need to be connected with a local church. I worry about folks who say they are members of the church "in the Spirit" but who are never present in the body. It is impossible to live an effective, powerful, Christian life if you are living in isolation. It's also impossible to be in true fellowship if you only associate with people like you. That's nothing more than a sanctified social club. Fellowship crosses lines and builds bridges; it doesn't build fences. You can't separate fellowship, friendship, faith, and faithfulness. These are essential for a healthy believer and a healthy church.

This church supported Paul financially. Giving and tithing are issues where far too many are in bondage to materialistic thinking. Giving is an act of thanksgiving. It's a response to grace, not based on feelings but on obedience. These men and women obeyed God and gave generously. Let's be honest here: you can't ask God to answer your prayers if you are robbing Him. We are stewards of any resources He gives. Until we understand that from the right perspective, we'll be hijacking God's purpose for our lives.

They also helped him in spreading the gospel. Instead of operating in silos, they approached every area of life with a singular focus for the sake of the gospel. When it comes to living with purpose as Christians, we must believe in and act on the necessity and urgency of the Great Commission.

Finally, the Philippians shared in Paul's sufferings. They were sensitive to circumstances and situations that could have negatively impacted the spreading of the gospel. They paid attention and weren't self-centered. Far too many churches are full of people filled with themselves. They've never died to their flesh, and they don't care about anything that doesn't personally affect them. I remember a preacher who wanted to see if his people were listening when he talked to them at the back door of the church. When they asked, "How are you doing, preacher?" he said, "I'm depressed. I have cancer, and they've given me six weeks to live." The people never heard a word and most mumbled, "Well, see you next week . . ." Ron always said, "When you share with others in their sufferings, in some way, the suffering is lessened and the joy is doubled." Are you purposefully sharing with someone in their sufferings?

OUR FUTURE IN CHRIST

In Philippians 1:6, the word *perfect* means "to carry it through" or "bring it to completion." What God starts, He finishes. He will accomplish His work, and nothing can stop Him. John Phillips wrote, "The Holy Spirit never loses sight of the end of His work. His work will not end until He has made us just like Jesus."[3]

The right perspective leads to the right attitude. Paul continues bragging on the church in verses 7 and 8: "For it is only right for me to feel this way about you all, because I have you in my heart, since both in my imprisonment and in the defense and confirmation of the gospel, you all are partakers of grace with me. For God is my witness, how I long for you all with the affection of Christ Jesus." The word *right* signifies the outgrowth of having led many of the Philippians to faith in Christ. While some at Corinth would have weighed on his mind, the church in Philippi brought joy to his heart.

These fellow brothers and sisters were not afraid of Paul's chains, even though identifying with him could have meant chains for them too. Note the words *defense* and *confirmation*. The first is the Greek word *apologia*, from which we get our English word *apologetics*. The latter is a legal term signifying a guarantee. This church was motivated to uphold the gospel as the guarantee of God's promise of eternal life to all who believed. They shared the same passion and perspective as the apostle.

Suddenly nostalgia seems to hit Paul like a wave the minute Epaphroditus shows up at the prison. The word *affection* in verse 8 speaks literally of the bowels. In the first century, they believed the intestines, stomach, and liver held the most-tender part of a person's emotions. The New English Bible translates this verse: "God knows how I long for you all, with the deep yearning of Christ Jesus himself." It's an expression of the depth of Paul's love for them. Memories of better days were flooding his mind.

This sort of vulnerability is difficult for most pastors and leaders. In my own ministry experience, there have been times when I've let my guard down with people who later turned to use it against me. I was too trusting, and they failed to understand that I'm human too. Vance Havner taught me that the balance is to have the hide of a rhinoceros and the heart of a lamb . . . and not get the two confused. Most of us are afraid to open up to others because we've been burned by too many church gossips. Nonetheless, church should be a place where we feel safe to share. The church needs to be known for grace, not gossip.

RIGHT PERSPECTIVE LEADS TO RIGHT PRAYING

If we have the right perspective and the right attitude, we will pray in the right way: "And this I pray, that your love may abound still more and more in real knowledge and all discernment" (v. 9). Love within limits knows where to draw the line. Love met with knowledge and discernment isn't gullible or naïve, nor does it fear correction or discipline. ". . . so that you may approve [examine, test] the things that are excellent, in order to be sincere [to be held up to the sun and tested in the light] and blameless until the day of Christ; having been filled with the fruit of righteousness which comes through Jesus Christ, to the glory and praise of God" (vv. 10–11). This kind of praying empowers us to believe the God for whom nothing is impossible. If we live out the reality of the truths contained in these few verses, we will see a mighty move of God in our midst. Imagine the impact of a body of believers praying for and living in the reality of such truth. In one of my previous books, I talked about how Don Miller taught me to put an H in front of impossible. When God's people pray, something impossible becomes HIMpossible.

If we want to see change in our homes, churches, and nation, we must have an intentional eternal perspective. History bears witness to this reality. Purposeful praying with a biblical perspective brings powerful change. By the middle of the nineteenth century, despite its growing wealth and material success, the United States was divided over slavery and had forgotten God. In this context, Jeremiah Lanphier started a prayer group in Manhattan—fewer than ten people at first. The group grew little by little each week until, in February of 1858, there were dozens of groups meeting, totaling several thousand men. More than a million people were saved in one year.[4]

By the turn of the century, with the country and the world again in need of revival, a global prayer movement began; groups met from Chicago to Korea, from Melbourne to India. But it all began in Wales among a few men with a burden for revival. That revival of 1904 spread to the whole world.[5]

What are we known for? What is your church's reputation in the community? Is it prayer? Hunger for revival? Unity? Clear, biblical perspective? Unfortunately, most churches are known for busy schedules and empty pews. Perspective is key, not just when you have support, but also when things go south and turn negative. In 2003 we birthed a revival conference called ReFRESH®. We've hosted more than thirty conferences in every region of this nation and have found a hunger for God among pastors and leaders who are weary in the battle. It's not the world that's beating them up—it's carnal people in the church! In the battle, we need to grab hold of the throne of grace and cry out to the Lord of our salvation.

Quite honestly, it's hard to keep a positive outlook when people are sucking the life out of you. How are we to keep a godly perspective and stay purposeful when it seems the world is against us? One of the secrets to the victorious life is learning how to handle opposition, survive personal attacks, and manage disappointments. Dreams can be crushed. Visions voted down. Hope diminished. If you lose the perspective of your purpose, the mind becomes a battlefield where dark, dangerous thoughts rage. Paul knew how to handle critics, circumstances, and cynics. Though his outlook was bleak, his perspective was filled with hope. Paul didn't march into Rome as a successful evangelist and church planter. He was led there under Roman guard. It may not have happened the way he expected, but he got there.

> Now I want you to know, brethren, that my circumstances have turned out for the greater progress of the gospel, so that my imprisonment in the cause of Christ has become well known throughout the whole praetorian guard and to everyone else, and that most of the brethren, trusting in the Lord because of my imprisonment, have far more courage to speak the word of God without fear. Some, to be sure, are preaching Christ even from envy and strife, but some also from good will; the latter do it out of love, knowing that I am appointed for the defense of the gospel; the former proclaim Christ out of selfish ambition rather than from pure motives, thinking to cause me distress in my imprisonment. What then? Only that in every way, whether in pretense or in truth, Christ is proclaimed; and in this I rejoice.
>
> Yes, and I will rejoice, for I know that this will turn out for my deliverance through your prayers and the provision of the Spirit of Jesus Christ, according to my earnest expectation and hope, that I will not be put to shame in anything, but that with all boldness, Christ

will even now, as always, be exalted in my
body, whether by life or by death. For to me, to
live is Christ and to die is gain. (Phil. 1:12–21)

How do you flip the table on negative circumstances? Is it possible to take the setbacks and turn them into platforms for God's glory? Yes! Joseph did it in his response to his brothers. Moses did it in the wilderness. Paul responded likewise to the thorn in the flesh. The great English preacher C. H. Spurgeon urged pastors to have a "blind eye and a deaf ear" when it came to gossip and criticism. He said, "You can't stop people's tongues and therefore the best thing to do is to stop your own ears and never mind what is spoken. . . . Judge it to be a small matter what men think or say of you and care only for their treatment of your Lord."[6]

Tacitus, the father-in-law of Julius Agricola, Roman governor of Britain, said Christians were "hated for their enormities."[7] Paul found himself on the receiving end of Roman justice, waiting for a verdict. Yet he never saw himself as a victim of circumstances or the system. Meanwhile, the response of others toward Paul reminds me of a twenty-four-hour news cycle. One minute you're hot, the next you're not. One minute you are leading the pack and then, in a flash, you're yesterday's news. I once heard Lehman Strauss say, "The formula for a blessed ministry is to simply preach, pray, and plug away." Paul was both loved and hated in his time. The people who are most often criticized are leaders. If you want to be a leader, expect criticism. True leaders are change agents. They will not settle for status quo. A. W. Tozer remarked, "Never be afraid of honest criticism. If the critic is wrong, you can help him; and if you're wrong, he can help you. Either way, somebody's helped."[8] Remember, you don't have to snuff out someone else's light for yours to shine.

Some were inspired by Paul to stand strong, seeing the strength of his faith. Others ridiculed him: "If he had more faith, he wouldn't be in prison." There were sects that hated the government and wanted to use him as a catalyst and excuse for verbal attacks on Rome. Those who opposed him within the church would exalt themselves at his expense. Regardless, Paul's perspective was clear. He wasn't concerned about their motives or their threats; his one concern was that Christ be preached. Stuart Briscoe wisely observed, "He had discovered that things happened *to* him in order that things should happen *in* him. And things happened *in* him so that things could happen *through* him."[9]

PURPOSEFUL PERSPECTIVE IN THE MIDST OF CRITICISM

Only by living purposefully and seeing the bigger picture can you have the right perspective. If you can gain God's perspective, you'll embrace the fact that delay is not denial. Like it or not, discomfort is part of God's plan. Most of us don't grow until we are pushed out of the crib, out of the box, and out of our comfort zone. We live in a fallen world. We will miss what God is trying to do in us if we try, at any cost, to avoid trials. Most of us like lemonade, but we don't often like to be squeezed. The better response is, "Lord, what do You want me to learn from this? How can I see You in this moment? Will I trust You in this to make me better, or will I become bitter?"

One way to deal with your critics and keep a spiritual perspective is to ask yourself a few questions about the criticism.

1. How was it given? Was it anonymous? Judgmental? Was it given in anger or in sincerity?
2. Where and when did you hear about it? Was it through social media? On a blog? In public or in private?
3. Why is it happening? Is it because someone is jealous? Is it because you need a little pruning in your life? Do you need to die to self?

Disappointments are a reality of life. There are no perfect homes, churches, or people. But we can turn to the Lord in our disappointment and seek how to be used to accomplish His purpose and plan. Yes, I'm sure Paul was frustrated while in prison. On the surface, time was wasting. No, he wasn't physically comfortable. During his life, the apostle bore many physical hardships for Christ. Some of the churches he planted disappointed him and even broke his heart. Everywhere he turned he faced opposition. But he kept a biblical point of view unto eternity.

The gospel is offensive. Lordship is confrontational. Purposeful people stand for what they believe in, regardless of the cost. As you read Paul's words in chapter 1, it might shock you to realize the people causing such grief were not the Jews who rejected Christ, nor the Greeks who thought the whole Christian thing was foolish, nor the pagans in the major cities of the Roman Empire. Paul's attackers were professing Christians who were preaching Christ! It's one thing to be attacked by the world and the devil. It's another thing to be blindsided or undermined by someone who claims to be a Christian.

I have a pastor friend who serves in the largest church in his community. He is often criticized by other pastors as his church consistently leads the region in baptisms and missions giving. Attacks often come from insecure pastors, jealous ministries, and people trying to promote their own agenda. Some pastors have intentionally targeted his church, trying to steal sheep instead of seeking to reach the lost. It's a sign of a competitive spirit if the success of your church is determined by how many people you can steal from another church. There's a world of difference in someone seeking to win people to Christ and someone seeking to win people to themselves.

Paul's critics were jealous of his success, yet in a prison cell, God was working to help him maintain a divine perspective. Paul never denied there were problems. He faced them, but he didn't dwell on them. Paul knew what we must learn: any issue, problem, or setback you experience has been authorized by God. It was true with Job, Joseph, the children in the wilderness, Peter, and countless others.

The difference between moving forward and wallowing in the situation is your attitude. "What then? Only that in every way, whether in pretense or in truth, Christ is proclaimed; and in this I rejoice" (v. 18). Paul was a man just like us. He got mad. Situations grieved him. He bled. He hurt. He was rejected. He was destructible but not destroyed. Far too many believers and leaders waste their lives either trying to be something they are not or trying to put others down to build themselves up. Paul had a different perspective. He determined that the message mattered more than the method. "Yes, and I will rejoice, for I know that this will turn out for my deliverance through your prayers and the provision of the Spirit of Jesus Christ" (vv. 18–19).

Notice again how prayers, perspective, and purpose are intertwined. Paul refers to the prayers of the saints *and* the provision of the Spirit. We need both. And don't miss the fact that he mentions the prayers of the saints before the provision of the Spirit. In the atmosphere of prayer, we gain perspective and become more likely to embrace the provisions of the Spirit.

CHOOSING CONTENTMENT

Although Paul might not be delivered physically from prison, he was confident of God delivering him from the temptation to fall into self-pity, frustration, anger, resentment, self-justification, and revenge. Paul was not a helpless victim of his circumstances; he was a man on a mission. Maybe you are bitter about the home you live in, or you don't like the school you attend. It could be you hate the town where you reside and think you deserve better. You've come to resent your situations and circumstances. Rather than trying to see what God might have in mind, you've turned inward and become self-absorbed. Is it possible that God may want you to pray something like this? "God, I don't like the fact that I'm _____. But You have me here for a reason. Show me my purpose. Open my eyes and ears to the people I need to speak to, the places where I need to serve, the calling You have on my life." If you don't begin to see yourself on mission, you're just going to be miserable for the rest of your life.

Regardless of what comes our way, life and death are not the main issue. Living and dying are secondary. Paul wasn't certain whether he would live or die, and that's the reason he could keep from getting hung up on these people. His one concern was to magnify Christ in his body. That motivated him, focused him, and empowered him for the battles. Whether we live or die is beside the point. The essential and eternal fact is simple: we are the Lord's. Unfortunately the facts often become clouded by our carnal expectations. We want certain favorable conditions and can even begin to believe God owes them to us. We like our prosperity. We will give God a nod, but not lay our lives on the altar. We tend to resist anything that requires a lifestyle adjustment. For example, the persecution of Christians around the world may sadden us, but not enough to pray for them or even to be willing to die ourselves for the cause of Christ. We are "concerned," but not enough to surrender our children to the Lord to follow His calling to an unnamed country and possibly martyrdom.

Paul was content no matter where he was. We can't control our circumstances or other people, and the vast majority of the things we deal with are out of our hands. This is where faith brings a biblical perspective. The only thing I can control is how I respond to what I can't control, and that response determines whether Christ is my life. Paul wanted God's name to be made great, visible, apparent, and obvious. We are to live in such a way that when others watch us, they see Christ magnified in our lives. Our prayer and purpose should be to reflect how big our God really is, turning the conversation from the trials and tribulations to the amazing grace of God.

It's not about being heard, but about making Christ known. It's not about being set free from our infirmities, but about displaying the hope of Christ to those who are lost and bound by sin. It's not about becoming known for doing a great work, but about many experiencing the life-changing power of the cross. George Duncan wrote,

> There may be qualities lacking in your life as a Christian that God can only secure if he puts you in a place utterly difficult, desperately lonely, when doubt beats in upon your soul, where jealousy is tending to thrust up its angry, ugly head, where resentment's fires are liable to burst into flame. That is the very place that is going to turn to your salvation. God is going to do something to you that will make you sweet and gracious and lovely. He cannot do it anywhere except in the fire, so he puts you there, where the difficult situation can turn to your greater salvation.[10]

Earlier, I mentioned one of the great principles Ron Dunn taught so many: "Good and evil run on parallel tracks, and they normally arrive about the same time." It's important to remember that they don't typically run consecutively, but concurrently. Paul was imprisoned and death was imminent. However, the good news of Christ was being preached in Caesar's household. If I live, it's Christ; if I die, it's more of Christ!

How's your perspective? Is it realistic? Is it biblical? Your kids may never get better. Your physical abilities will fail. Your marriage may not be restored. Your finances may never turn around. Things you wish would change may not. The great danger in this reality is we can begin to see only the bad and forget the good. We see the snares and forget the times when we were delivered from the snare. Can you hear Paul saying, "I may be martyred tomorrow, but it will end up being better than where I am today"? Bitterness didn't blind him. The pioneer had become a prisoner, but he wasn't bound up in his problems. Neither did he let the fact that God was blessing others in their ministry—even others who spoke ill of him—cause him to be jealous.

When I was younger, I felt idealistically invincible. As the realities of life set in, my ideals were often shattered. I remember sitting in Vance Havner's living room about nine months before he died. I was in the early days of my ministry, seeking to impress my mentor and hero. He was sitting in a rocking chair, and I was sitting on the couch leaning in toward him. Finally, he put his hand on my arm and said, "Now son, I've been young and I've been old. You've just been young. Why don't you listen to me for a while." I gained a new perspective on ministry just by listening and being teachable that day.

As a young man, I would often default into finding my purpose in numbers—attendance and responses. Although Dr. Havner had been pouring into my life since my early days in college, it really wasn't until that moment that the lightbulb turned on and I realized ministries can't always be evaluated by outward signs and things we often boast about. Rather our "success" in ministry is in being available to God and obedient to His call. It's not size but sort.

God does not waste our experiences. Warren Wiersbe notes, "We know that nothing we do for Him will ever be wasted or lost. We can be steadfast in our service, unmovable in suffering, abounding in ministry to others, because we know our labor is not in vain."[11] Keep your hands to the plow. Be steadfast and immovable. Maintain the eternal perspective because what you do matters.

Gary Miller defines a man's prayer as "an expression of his earnest expectation of being heard, and an absolute assurance of his deliverance by the hand of Sovereign God."[12] When we live with a purposeful perspective based in prayer, it keeps us in the battle. No matter what happens, this is not resignation—it is realization.

CHAPTER 4

THE POWER OF PURPOSE
Philippians 1:18–21

The two greatest days in a person's life are the day he was born and the day he finds out why he was born.
—Anonymous

A. W. TOZER wrote, "God made us for himself; that is the first and last thing that can be said about human existence and whatever more we add is but commentary."[1] Not only are we created in the image of God, but we have a God-given purpose for living. Life is not random wandering until we run into death in the end; we are called to live on purpose.

If we are not careful, we will lose our sense of purpose. Circumstances, people-pleasing, past mistakes, unconfessed sin, our flesh, and Satan himself can all derail us and cause us to miss God's best for our lives. But what if I told you that, no matter what, you can live a life on purpose? That I've found the secret to living at the highest possible level with the maximum results? Would you be curious? Would you stop everything to pursue it?

When I was a youth minister, I spent a lot of time talking to students about God's will for their lives. More often than not, those conversations were about college or career choices. However, I always wanted to help them see the bigger picture. God is not as concerned about a person's college of choice or their career as He is their relationship with Him. It is in the heart of God to have intimate communion with His children. He wants us to know Him and live in the power of that relationship.

Paul was certainly missing his God-ordained purpose prior to his encounter with Christ. Sincere? Yes. Fervent and passionate about his calling? Absolutely. Committed? To a fault. But he was going fast in the wrong direction! It took a confrontation with the living Lord on the road to Damascus to get Paul on the right path. I believe that encounter so changed him that he could have written Philippians 1:21 the minute he got his sight back.

EVERYBODY WANTS A PURPOSE

Purpose is revolutionary and liberating. It gives clarity and infuses us with the ability to prioritize our lives. Purpose is different than vision. Everyone has a vision, but not everyone has a purpose. Vision can simply be a dream; purpose is intentional. Shawn Lovejoy writes about vision:

> Vision statements are a dime a dozen as far as I'm concerned. Everyone these days has a vision statement. A few years ago, everyone had a "2020 Vision." Soon it will be a "2050 Vision," and so on. At the end of the day, however, a vision statement is just a *statement*. It has no life on its own. It cannot, nor will it ever, energize, unify, or align an organization. This task falls to the leader. A vision statement is only as strong as the leader is. Vision is only as clear as the leader is. Vision is only as compelling as a leader makes it.[2]

Several years ago, Rick Warren's *Purpose Driven Life* became one of the best-selling books of any genre in history. It struck a chord in the hearts of people around the world and was translated into dozens of languages. Across denominational lines, people were reading, studying, and preaching about this concept of purpose. Warren had clearly hit a nerve, and people wanted a sense of purpose and meaning. He expanded the purpose-driven idea as it pertains to the church and developed this slogan: "A great commitment to the Great Commandment and the Great Commission will grow a great church."[3] That one statement encompasses the ministries of evangelism, discipleship, fellowship, and missions. The message of that book still resonates with me today. And I want it to be part of our DNA at Sherwood.

GOSPEL PURPOSE

Where do we find the power of purpose in Scripture? As you read the Gospels, it is clear that Jesus purposefully healed the sick and taught the multitudes. He intentionally went to Samaria. He set His face toward Jerusalem as the time of His crucifixion drew near. Jesus didn't run from His purpose; He fulfilled it. When you know the time is short, you can't afford to waste it—Jesus established a worldwide ministry in three and a half years! Since we are His followers and have no promise of our next breath, let alone our next twenty years, shouldn't we live with the same sense of purpose?

Not long ago on a trip to Israel, I walked along the path Jesus and the disciples would have taken from Nazareth into Galilee through the Valley of the Doves on the northern side of the Sea of Galilee. As Jesus and the disciples approached the Sea, they would have often stopped at the village of Magdala, located at the end of the valley. In recent years they've uncovered the first-century synagogue in Magdala. We know according to the Scriptures that Jesus preached in the synagogues in this region, and He would have preached in this one. He purposely went to the synagogues as a testimony in the flesh of the fulfillment of all God's promises. As Paul began to share the gospel, he would also go first to the synagogue in each town or city and proclaim that Jesus was the fulfillment of the prophecies related to Messiah. Though at times neither Jesus nor Paul was welcomed by the religious crowd, they nonetheless intentionally took the truth to them.

Paul had a vision driven by a clear purpose: to reach the world with the gospel. It resulted in various difficulties, trials, and opposition in every city . . . yet he never wavered. Why? His purpose drove his vision. Even when others wanted to hinder or derail him, he kept going. Even prison couldn't stop him from following God's plan for his life.

> What then? Only that in every way, whether in pretense or in truth, Christ is proclaimed; and in this I rejoice. Yes, and I will rejoice, for I know that this will turn out for my deliverance through your prayers and the provision of the Spirit of Jesus Christ, according to my earnest expectation and hope, that I will not be put to shame in anything, but that with all boldness, Christ will even now, as always, be exalted in my body, whether by life or by death. For to me, to live is Christ and to die is gain. (Phil. 1:18–21)

George Mitchell, in his book *Chained and Cheerful*, writes, "Here is the Christ-intoxicated man, giving an unashamed testimony which separates him from the kind of preachers he has been writing about."[4] Gary Miller notes, "Paul was held in high esteem by some, undermined by others, betrayed by a few, and today is remembered by millions. His focus in life was on making a difference, not making a name for himself."[5]

The Christ-life is obviously about living—living now and living in eternity with Christ. In the days of the early church, Tertullian invited pagans to watch how Christians lived and how they died. When you read *Foxe's Book of Martyrs* and similar books, you realize that the average American has no clue how to deal with conflict, opposition, adversity, or dying.

Paul's statement in verse 21 seems simple, yet it is so profound and volumes have been written regarding his words. Because of Twitter and other social media outlets, we have learned to sum up our thoughts in a limited number of characters. On Twitter, users have to make their point in 140 characters or less, requiring creative abbreviations and, oftentimes, a lot of poor grammar! What if you had to summarize your life, your sermon, your Bible study lesson, or even your epitaph in twelve words or less? It would certainly make you focus and examine your purpose carefully. How can a person sum up their day, their life, their ministry, their career or their family in one sentence? Paul did it, and his words summarize the Christian life for all of us, bringing laser focus to our reason for living.

While millions of books have been written and countless sermons have been preached on the Christian life, Paul says it all in a few words that often find themselves on plaques, prints, and cards: "For to me, to live is Christ, and to die is gain." In this one verse you find the full explanation, the essence of the Christian life. How would you fill in the blank? For to me to live is what? A career? Fame? Money? Family? Retirement? And what about the second part of the verse? "To die is _____." The reality is that if living is anything other than Christ, dying is a loss. The power of purpose begins in knowing what you are living for and why.

Jesus addressed this with the disciples when He talked to them about abiding: ". . . for apart from Me you can do nothing" (John 15:5). Zero. Zip. Apart from Christ, nothing eternally significant happens. Paul wrote in another letter that the works of many would burn up like wood, hay, and straw (see 1 Cor. 3:10–15). So let's think about this. What would it mean to remain here on earth to enjoy the pleasures of this world versus departing from this life to spend eternity united with Christ?

To remain on earth would mean to stay in his temporary residence, but to depart would be to go home. To remain on earth would be suffering *and* joy; to depart would be pure joy. To remain on earth would be to remain in the battle and absent from the Lord; to depart would be a feast in the presence of the Lord. To remain would be Christ; to depart would be more of Christ.

For Paul, the choice would have been easy on a personal level. However, the Philippians needed him, and the concerns of the church weighed heavy on his heart. If we're not careful, we can live life selfishly and consider only our personal comforts and desires. Paul's letters are constant reminders that we are to live for Jesus and others. That almost sounds like a foreign language in our self-absorbed culture.

Look at the context of the apostle's powerful statement. Paul sets it up by declaring that the great purpose of his life was for Christ to be magnified in his body. In his everyday life, whether preaching or tent making, Paul wanted his conduct, behavior, attitude, and actions to make much of Jesus. Magnifying Jesus is bigger than bumper stickers, hashtags, pictures on social media, or Christian T-shirts. It's about who we are at the core of our being. The Holy Spirit who lives within us lives His life out through us so that when people see us, they see Christ.

Ron Dunn remarked, "You have to be right in your purpose. I'm talking about the absorbing purpose in your life. Many of us have lesser purposes, of lesser degrees, and lesser grades. We have to have these, but that's not what I'm talking about. I'm talking about the all-absorbing purpose in our life, because whatever that all-absorbing purpose is, that purpose takes every other circumstance and bends it to its service. It makes every other circumstance a servant of the purpose."[6]

CONVICTION, NOT CONVENIENCE

Purpose has nothing to do with convenience; it has everything to do with convictions. It isn't about popularity; it's about finding why God put you on this planet. Purpose can't be altered by unfavorable circumstances. I see this too often in ministry. Some men go into the ministry thinking it's an easy job, and when they face pressure, criticism, or even firing, they suddenly change their calling.

Eric Liddell is a name most often associated with running. His life was displayed on the big screen in the film *Chariots of Fire*, and he has been heralded a hero. Son of missionaries to China, Eric was heavily involved in both running and rugby, but chose to devote more of his time to the former. He took home gold and bronze medals in the Paris Olympics and then returned to China where he served as a missionary from 1925 to 1943. Life became quite dangerous, and his wife and children fled to Canada while Eric stayed behind. In 1943, he was taken to the Japanese internment camp in Weihsien where he died in 1945, five months prior to the camp's liberation by American airmen.

A friend to many, Liddell left behind a legacy of humility, passion, and purpose. *The Student*, Edinburgh University's magazine, wrote of him in December 1923:

> Ninety-nine men, gifted with Eric's prowess, would now be insufferably swollen headed, but here we have the hundredth man. Here is a man who hates praise and shuns publicity, yet is deserving of both. Here is a man with a mind of his own, and not afraid to voice his most secret feeling on a platform if, by doing so, he thinks it will help his fellows. Here is a man who has courage, and delights to accept a challenge, be it for the sake of his School, his

Varsity, his country or his God. And lastly, here
is a man who wins because he sets his teeth,
quietly but firmly, and always plays the game.
Everyone is fond of Eric.

Eric Liddell rightly recognized that his life was not about
him; it was about his God. His vision for running and his passion for Christ fueled his fight in an eternal race that Liddell
finished with valor and integrity.

In his book, *It's Not About Me*, Max Lucado writes about
this truth that Liddell knew so well:

The God-centered life works. And it rescues
me from a life that doesn't. . . . If it's not about
me, does God care about me? God's priority
is his glory. He occupies center stage; I carry
props. He's the message; I'm but a word. . . . If
it's all about you, then it's all up to you. . . . I
believe Satan trains battalions of demons to
whisper one question in our ears: "What are
people thinking of you?"[7]

Paul wanted people to focus on Christ. The message was
Christ, and Paul lived to share that message with the world.
Nothing mattered to Paul more than the gospel. He was simply
a slave, servant, the chief of sinners. Yes, he was also an apostle,
but he didn't throw his title around trying to get a ministe-
rial discount or the praise of men. God empowers the kind of
life He expects. We can't live the Christ-filled life in our own

strength—it's impossible. At the core, Christianity is a person, not a program, method, rules, or regulations. Christianity is the life of Christ in the believer.

It's a breakthrough when we gain a true understanding that the Christian life is *in* Christ. The indwelling Christ makes life meaningful, purposeful, and powerful. As one preacher said, "There is no demand made on my life that is not a demand on the life of Christ in me." God is not looking for my help. I'm in desperate need of His help, and I can't live out His purpose in my power.

Years ago, it dawned on me: God doesn't expect anything from my flesh except failure. If I could fulfill God's purpose in my flesh, I wouldn't need Christ's blood to save me or His Spirit to fill me. When faced with impossible situations, the late Stephen Olford used to say, "Over to You, Jesus." He would surrender himself and the situation to Jesus. Christ in me is the grace, self-control, kindness, meekness, and power that I need to glorify Him in my body. Over time, we've so watered down Christianity that we constantly have to come up with adjectives or phrases to describe what it really is. We call it the exchanged life, the deeper life, the Spirit-filled life, the Christ-controlled life. No matter what terminology you use, it's the life of Christ in and through us. When we grasp this reality, it changes our perspective. How can anyone really say with confidence, "For to me, to live is Christ and to die is gain"? Because the moment we gave our hearts and lives to Christ, His Holy Spirit came to take up permanent residence in us. He is our resource. As we abide in Him, the abundant and abiding life becomes a reality.

Having a purpose is powerful. And it's also practical. One of the most damaging philosophies I find today is the compartmentalization of faith. For some reason people buy the lie that the life of Christ operates in a vacuum or a silo. What Christ does and wants to do is separated from real life. It works on Sunday, but it's not effective and efficient for Monday through Saturday. Nothing could be further from the truth. Until we see God as the source and sustainer, we'll never have the life we could have in Christ. We must understand that purpose requires clarity. We aren't sick; we're dead. We don't need a crutch; we need a resurrection. Our only hope for this life and the next is the life of Christ.

This gives each believer purpose in the everyday experiences of life. How we live, how we relate to others, our work ethic, our family life, our view of money—it all comes under living for Christ. For Paul, that even included imprisonment. People grew in their faith and were emboldened to spread the gospel as they read of his response to adversity. The opponents of Paul thought they would stress him out because he was imprisoned and couldn't address them personally. They had selfish, carnal motives for their ministry. But Paul was clear: *all of this*—the injustice, unfair treatment, imprisonment—would turn out for his deliverance (spiritual welfare). Purpose allows a person to rest in the sovereignty of God.

When I was growing up, I worked in my dad's drugstore from the age seven. Every day after school, I went to the store to work until closing. My dad gave me a strong work ethic. I started at twenty-five cents an hour, and Dad would take out my tithe and then put another ten percent in savings. Thus he taught me to value a job, give my first and best to God, and always prepare for a rainy day. While I learned the value of hard work from my dad, I didn't find a purpose in what I was doing. It was a job, not a calling. My father had hoped I would grow up and be a pharmacist like him, but when I told him God called me to the ministry, he was supportive. He sacrificed so that I could go to a Christian college and seminary. He didn't have the money, but he wanted to enable me to do what God had called me to do. Sadly, I think my dad settled for less than the best, for just trying to make a living, pay the bills, and own a home. He didn't take a vacation for more than thirty years. It destroyed his health, and he missed out on so many things. Life is more than existing, breathing, working, and then dying.

Nonetheless, I'm grateful for these life lessons because I've carried them into the ministry. Even more than the work ethic, Dad taught me what customer service should look like and how to go above and beyond. He taught me to pay attention to details. Almost every day of my life, the practical things I learned from my dad find their way into my life and ministry. I knew I didn't want to spend the rest of my life in a drugstore, and God had another purpose for me. Sometimes, people think going into the ministry will fix all their problems, but they have the wrong view of serving God.

One reason the gospel is not impacting our culture is because too many believers are whining about their circumstances. We complain about "first-world problems" like not having the latest technology, while third-world Christians are losing their lives. We face a small setback or minor suffering, and we start to gripe. We want a new job, a new life, a better house, and on and on because we think purpose is found in stuff or feelings. We never find Paul asking God to change his circumstances so he could be a better believer. He doesn't pray, "Lord, if You'll get me out of this prison, I'll be a better Christian. I'll serve You like never before." He doesn't pray for his release or even indicate a desire for it.

I, on the other hand, would be writing letters to my congressman or finding a lawyer to sue the folks who put me in jail. I'd probably write a blog about those mean people undermining my good intentions, all while singing "Poor, poor pitiful me!" Certainly I would call the church and ask them to start a prayer chain or, better yet, an all-night prayer meeting. Why didn't Paul respond this way? Because although he was chained, the Word of God was not.

Remember his "earnest expectation" in verse 20? The term means to watch for something with your head turned away from everything else. It's a picture of intense concentration that ignores every other interest. Paul's intense desire was that Christ, in every way, shape, and form, would be magnified in his body. Whether he lived or died. Whether he was imprisoned or set free. For the apostle, the issue was never living or dying; the issue was that Christ be magnified. His goal was Christ. His focus was Christ. He wanted everyone who was watching him—the guards, his enemies, his friends—to see the greatness of God in his life regardless of the situation.

In the best-selling book *The One Thing*, author Gary Keller writes, "I looked back at my successes and failures and discovered an interesting pattern. Where I'd had huge success, I had narrowed my concentration to one thing, and where my success varied, my focus had too." Keller goes on to ask how, although everyone has the same number of hours in a day, some people accomplish more. "They go small. . . . 'Going small' is ignoring all the things you could do and doing what you should do. It's recognizing that not all things matter equally and finding the things that matter most."[8]

Paul went small in a sense. He had a narrow focus. "For me to live is Christ. . . . This is the one thing I do." We do so little because we try to do so much and please so many people. One preacher admitted, "I lived on Sunday in the Spirit, and I lived Monday through Saturday in the flesh. I had to have the anointing and filling of the Spirit to preach. But Monday through Saturday, out of the pulpit, I was living in the flesh." Let's be honest—that describes more people than just preachers.

What's your purpose? If it's merely to make money, then everything in life will be about how to make even more. If it's your hobby, then everything will be about how to become a better hunter, fisherman, or athlete. If it's fitness and beauty, then you'll become obsessed with your outward appearance and will do whatever necessary to keep a youthful look. In the end, all of these will disappoint and will ultimately fade away.

Paul's purpose seems light years removed from what we see in the American church and the American family today. Let me say something as a pastor who has observed "church folks" for more than forty years. I've known countless people who think nothing of missing church, not tithing, and never serving or witnessing. They attend, but they aren't "all in." How can they do that and not feel guilty or motivated to change? Because their all-consuming purpose has never been to live for Christ. Christ is an additive, but He is not life. He's one of many interests, but not the one and only God. Their life's purpose has nothing to do with Christ at all.

If Christ isn't our all-consuming purpose, eventually we are slaves to circumstances, feelings, and events. Paul could live for Christ anywhere: in prison before the carnal Corinthians, in the face of Gnostics and Judaizers, before governors and kings and soldiers, in the middle of a shipwreck, after being beaten. Anywhere. Everywhere. Isn't it time we learned to say, "Good or bad, I'm going to view my circumstances as an opportunity to magnify Christ and to show the world that Christ is my life"?

Look at Paul's second letter to the Corinthians:

> But we have this treasure [talking about Jesus]
> in earthen vessels [our body], so that the sur-
> passing greatness of the power will be of God
> and not from ourselves; we are afflicted in
> every way, but not crushed; perplexed, but not
> despairing; persecuted, but not forsaken; struck
> down, but not destroyed; always carrying about
> in the body the dying of Jesus, so that the life
> of Jesus also may be manifested in our body.
> For we who live are constantly being delivered

over to death for Jesus' sake, so that the life of Jesus also may be manifested in our mortal flesh. (2 Cor. 4:7–11)

PREPARING FOR DEATH WITH A PURPOSE

How do you view death? Are you scared of it? Do you do all you can to avoid talking about it? Are you so fearful that you haven't even made a will? No one lives forever. We are all going to die of something, at some point in time. Paul wasn't scared to die; he looked forward to it in anticipation of being joined to Christ. Jesus said in John 14:6, "I am the way, and the truth, and the life." Jesus is the source and meaning of real life. If He is the way, then every other way is the wrong way. If He is the truth, then all other "truth" is either relative or based on faulty information or a distorted worldview. If He is the life, then all other so-called lives lead to death and destruction. Jesus is the source of all that is meaningful—in the cosmic sense of energy, in the moral sense of truth, in the practical sense of direction for living, and in the origin of spiritual vitality. Charles Baskerville writes, "Christ Jesus must be the origin of life, the essence of life, the aim of life, the solace of life and the reward of life."[9] If that's not our reality, then death is a tragic loss and life has no purpose or meaning.

Paul was ready for life or death. He had his house in order. He wasn't just marking time or following a program. His life had been and would continue to be lived in Christ until he was with Christ. Life or death, Paul was ready. He had no desire to be a worthless worker in a world of work, nor did he want to be a fruitless tree that had long outlived its days of productivity. His attitude was, if there's work left to be done, let me get on with it. If not, I'm ready to see Jesus.

Paul's perspective was profitable. The word for *gain* in verse 21 is a bookkeeping term. For Paul, death was just cashing in on the principle and interest of the investment he had made in Christ and the investment Christ had made in him. Death brings us more of Christ. Death would not be an end or an interruption. It was continuing in a new dimension. Everything that was good and godly would still be there. The change from life to death was clearly a gain. "Nothing was to be dropped but what it was progress to lose, and whatever was kept was to be heightened."

The Bible tells us to set our hearts and affections on things above (see Col. 3:2). The late Associate evangelist Joseph D. Blinco said, "To believe in heaven is not to run away from life; it is to run toward it." Paul's perspective was, "If I live, I'm going to keep on preaching and planting churches. If I die, I get to see Jesus face to face. Either way, it's a great deal."

If I don't have a purpose for living that is eternal, then dying is a tragedy. Paul had a balanced perspective about living and dying. "But if I am to live on in the flesh, this will mean fruitful labor for me; and I do not know which to choose. But I am hard-pressed from both directions, having the desire to depart and be with Christ, for that is very much better" (Phil. 1:22–23).

Paul was ready, but he was also a realist. He knew that if he were to depart, it might, at that moment, have a negative impact on all the young, immature churches he had established. The needs of others always weighed on his heart. He was ready to die, but at the same time, he knew if he stayed, he could keep writing, teaching, discipling, and developing churches and leaders. He was always aware of the work still to be done. Richard Baxter wrote a seventeenth-century hymn titled "Lord, It Belongs Not to My Care," which he started with these words: "Lord, it belongs not to my care whether I die or live; to love and serve Thee is my share. And that Thy grace must give."

The word *depart* is important. It's a nautical term that refers to sailors preparing a ship to depart by loosening it from the moorings so it could set sail. I remember growing up on the coast and watching massive ships leave the local shipyard. They would sail off until they disappeared over the horizon. They left our port, but eventually arrived at another. We would stand on the shore and say, "There she goes," and at the destination point they would say, "Here she comes." The word is also used as a military term. It can mean to pull up stakes on a tent or to strike the tent. When the battle is over and the army is moving on, they strike the tent and depart. Another use of the term is for the release of a prisoner when he is set free to go home. Paul would have been looking for the day when his battles were over and he was free to go to his heavenly home.

To die is gain when we understand we are headed for a place that has been built by the hands of a sovereign, loving, heavenly Father. Its foundations, walls, and decorations are all that the omniscient mind of God could conceive and the omnipotent hand of God could prepare for His children. "Things which eye has not seen and ear has not heard, and which have not entered the heart of man, all that God has prepared for those who love Him" (1 Cor. 2:9).

Adrian Rogers once preached a sermon on "Getting Ready for Heaven," in which he talked about why death is gain:

1. The Person to whom it takes us
2. The place to which it brings us
3. The provision with which it affords us (Matt. 5:12; 6:20; Phil. 1:22; Rev. 14:13)
4. The people with whom it unites us (Matt. 8:11; 1 Pet. 1:8)

Christ is the only thing that keeps death from being loss. Whatever is not of Christ is loss; thus, for the believer, death is no longer an enemy. In fact, the gospel makes death our servant, for it is through death that we are ushered into the presence of Christ.

My friend Ron Dunn walked in the fullness of the Spirit although he suffered from depression. He lived above his circumstances in a way that always made me marvel. The last year of Ron's life was very painful. He was suffering physically, unable to travel and speak for months on end. His lungs were hardening and scarring. For months, they didn't know what was wrong with him, and he was actually diagnosed while at Sherwood preaching a conference the September before he died.

At one point while Ron was in the hospital and things were not going well, he asked his wife, Kaye, to stay with him. He said, "I'm afraid if you go, I'll never see you again." After a while, Ron said, a peace came over him. Ron (who had an incredible sense of humor and sarcasm) said, "Maybe it was the dope I was on—that was good stuff—but I believe it was the Lord. I stopped crying. I knew I was going to die, but I had no fear of it. I knew that death would only serve me better and bring me into the presence of the Lord."

For to me to live is Christ . . . and to die is gain.

CHAPTER 5

PURPOSEFUL CONSISTENCY
Philippians 1:27–30

If I were a non-Christian and dropped into the average church during a so-called revival, and saw a fraction of the membership trying to get more recruits for the army of the Lord when most of the outfit had already gone AWOL, I would conclude either that Christianity is not what it is supposed to be or else we have been sold a cheap and easy brand—inoculated with a mild form until we are almost immune to the real thing.

—Vance Havner

IN THE CLASSIC devotional book *My Utmost for His Highest*, Oswald Chambers includes a chapter titled, "The Secret of Spiritual Consistency." Chambers writes:

> When a person is newly born again, he seems inconsistent due to his unrelated emotions and the state of the external things or circumstances in his life. The apostle Paul had a strong and steady underlying consistency in his life. Consequently, he could let his external life change without internal distress because he was rooted and grounded in God. Most of us are not consistent spiritually because we are more concerned about being consistent externally. In the external expression of things, Paul lived in the basement, while his critics lived on the upper level. And these two levels do not begin to touch each other. But Paul's consistency was down deep in the fundamentals. The great basis of his consistency was the agony of God in the redemption of the world, namely, the Cross of Christ.[1]

No one knows who or what they can count on these days. When I was growing up, you could count on your Sunday school teacher to be there. Now it seems even church leaders look for ways to get away. When my parents bought an appliance, it lasted for twenty years and they never had a warranty. Terri and I are on our third dishwasher since we bought our current house less than ten years ago, and we've called for countless repairs to each one. We've learned to buy the warranty if we want to have enough money to retire.

WHOM CAN YOU COUNT ON?

It's hard to find consistency these days. Consistency means to be "marked by harmony, regularity, or steady continuity; free from variation or contradiction; showing steady conformity to character, profession, belief, or custom."[2] The very nature of Christianity demands consistency. The key to a consistent life is the indwelling of the Spirit and accountability. If we want to be relevant in this world, we can't be up and down in our Christian walk.

When I think about the power of a consistent life, I think of parenting. Parents need to agree on what's important. Parents have the privilege and responsibility to invest in raising their children in the "nurture and admonition of the Lord." A good parent can tell the difference between a mistake and intentional disobedience. Parents are like shepherds, nudging their sheep along the path. When I was a child, my parents expected me to behave. I heard statements like, "Act like you're somebody," "I better not catch you messing up," "Don't be running around like a chicken with your head cut off," "Mind your manners," and "Say yes sir and no sir and please and thank you." Manners have to be learned, so repetition is important for parents. Some parents fail to practice consistency in teaching manners. They fail to properly instruct or correct wrong behavior, and the end result is often a wayward child.

The same ideas apply to being a minister. I feel like I'm constantly reminding people how they should behave. While we all have to die daily, work on maintaining our walk with God, and grow as disciples, surely we don't need to be reminded to pick up our spiritual clothes, wash our spiritual hands, and have a godly temperament at every turn. I understand this with a new believer, but I do not understand it or accept it in someone who has been saved for years or even decades. Modeling Christlikeness should be the norm. I've served the same church for nearly thirty years. I've watched some people absorb truth like a sponge. They just can't get enough of God and are constantly learning and growing. Then there are those who come occasionally on a Sunday morning but give no evidence of any life change. They sit, soak, and sour. They seem to live in a negative frame of mind and complain that Christianity doesn't "work" for them. I would submit that it doesn't work because they haven't tried it.

Sporadic saints aren't purposeful or productive. Like the prodigal, they squander their inheritance in the pigpen of life. Paul certainly had his share of dealing with wayward, carnal, inconsistent believers. When the apostle was away, some would go off track and begin listening to false teachers or start acting foolishly. Numerous times he had to rebuke a church or remind them of what being a church and a believer looked like. Jesus addressed this issue in the book of Revelation where He had to rebuke five of the seven churches to "repent or else."

Left to ourselves . . . well, that's the problem. Left to ourselves we usually mess up. If you're ever in a store and hear

"Clean up on Aisle 7," don't always assume it was a child. There have been times when I wanted to get on a microphone and say, "Clean up in the Men's Bible study class," or "Clean up in the leadership at level two." The Corinthians resented Paul's rebuke. They assumed they could do anything they wanted and allowed sin to run rampant in the church without trying to stop it. Church discipline was not in their vocabulary. Let's be honest—there are some churches that are so bad, they need to take the name off their sign. They give the rest of us a bad name. Among the Philippians, Paul knew there were people trying to undermine the work of God in their hearts. He was determined to address this.

Whether you are in a family or a church, there are always going to be relationship issues. We are all sinners. Salvation gives us the grace to deal with issues instead of sweeping them under the rug. Life is about relationships. Some of us grew up in strong families and churches, and some of us grew up on the corner of Dysfunctional Drive and Panic Point. Family reunions are like having your wisdom teeth pulled. Some churches seem to exist to fight and fuss, split and attack each other. This is not what Christ had in mind. The inconsistent witness of an individual believer or of a church body is a damaging witness. Trust me, every lost person in town can tell you stories about carnal Christians they know and ugly churches. The devil makes sure the word gets out when God's people aren't acting like God's people.

The great pastor Gardner Taylor once preached a message where he said, "There is really no other way to find a sustaining faith except in personal venture. . . . The Bible is replete with almost unbelievably rich promises, but almost all of them are built upon some condition which we must fulfill. . . . There is a call to action which rings like a trumpet on almost every page of the New Testament."[3]

Alexander Maclaren, an incredible preacher of a former era, wrote,

> I believe, dear brethren, that modern Christianity has far too much lost the vivid impression of this present Christ as actually dwelling and working among us. What is good in us and what is bad in us conspire to make us think more of the past work of an ascended Christ than of the present work of an indwelling Christ. . . . If we are a Church of Christ at all, we have Christ in every deed among us, and working through us and on us. And unless we have, in no mystical and unreal and metaphorical sense, but in the simplest and yet grandest prose reality, that living Saviour here in our hearts and in our fellowship, better that these walls were leveled with the ground, and this congregation scattered to the four winds of Heaven. The present Christ is the life of His Church.[4]

THE POWER OF CHRISTIAN CONSISTENCY

This lack of consistency explains why churches lack power and Christians act like the lost. If we aren't consistent, we will miss out on the purpose of Christ in our lives and communities. God will not entrust great power to people who want to control the switch. He will not give us an abiding awareness of the Holy Spirit if we compartmentalize our faith.

I don't believe the average follower of Christ fully understands that, more than their pastor's preaching, it is their individual lives that will determine the depth of the church and the expansion of the gospel. If the preacher is calling people to the heights of faith but the people are living contrary to that call, which of the two do you think is likely to win that tug of war? Paul is tugging at the hearts of the Philippians to listen and do according to all he has instructed them. On this subject, Vance Havner wrote the following:

> In the light of God's picture of the times, in the urgency and emergency of a world hastening to disaster, surely, if ever the church ought to live with loins girded and lamps burning, praying and preaching with the light of another world in her eyes, it is today. Over and over we are exhorted to awake, to watch and pray, to exhort one another, and so much the more as we see the day approaching.[5]

BELIEF AND BEHAVIOR

What we believe determines how we behave. Go back to thinking about parenting. Have your children ever embarrassed you by their behavior? Let's get even more personal . . . have you ever embarrassed yourself? Now, let me ask the greater question: have we embarrassed God by our behavior? Have we hindered the advance of the gospel? If we lack consistency, don't we limit what God can do in and through us? Aren't we sending the wrong message to a lost world? I'm not talking about perfection, but direction. None of us are perfect, but all of us who know Christ have a power in us that is "greater than he that is in the world."

Paul wrote,

> Only conduct yourselves in a manner worthy of the gospel of Christ, so that whether I come and see you or remain absent, I will hear of you that you are standing firm in one spirit, with one mind striving together for the faith of the gospel; in no way alarmed by your opponents—which is a sign of destruction for them, but of salvation for you, and that too, from God. For to you it has been granted for Christ's sake, not only to believe in Him, but also to suffer for His sake, experiencing the same conflict which you saw in me, and now hear to be in me. (Phil. 1:27–30)

You don't have to be a Greek scholar to understand these words. Paul is clear that belief and behavior are tied together. These words reinforce how we are to act and react as we go through life. Leading up to these verses, Paul talked about his chains (vv. 12–14), his critics (vv. 15–19), and his crisis (vv. 20–26). Now he gives a command in the closing verse of this first chapter (vv. 27–30). He has moved from exultation to exhortation. Larry Crabb notes, "Far too many Christians do not deal honestly with their lives. Clichés about the power of the Word are repeated with smug piety among people who see little evidence of its life-changing impact . . . the pathway to change is more often discussed and debated than displayed."[6]

Don't read too quickly past the word *only* in verse 27. Paul is saying, "Meanwhile, whatever happens, above all . . ." Wuest notes, "Our God-ordained or God-permitted circumstances are used of God to provide for a pioneer advance of the gospel in our Christian service."[7] John Eadie notes Paul as saying, "My impressions being as I have described them, this one or sole thing would I enjoin upon you in the meanwhile."[8] In other words, as a citizen of heaven, while you are on earth, live like you're a citizen of heaven. As Ron Dunn always said, "Christians are people of the only."

PURPOSEFUL UNITY

Although the Philippians had a model church, they always had to stand against disruptive disunity. Why? Because unity is a lifestyle worthy and exemplary of the gospel. The Philippians were Roman citizens living in a Roman colony. The dialect of Rome was evident when you walked the streets of the city of Philippi. Paul stressed the point that they were citizens of heaven with their feet firmly planted on earth. This same dual citizenship is true in our lives, and it should be evident to those around you. What does this dual citizenship look like? It looks like walking in the Spirit:

> For what the Law could not do, weak as it was through the flesh, God did: sending His own Son in the likeness of sinful flesh and as an offering for sin, He condemned sin in the flesh, so that the requirement of the Law might be fulfilled in us, who do not walk according to the flesh but according to the Spirit. For those who are according to the flesh set their minds on the things of the flesh, but those who are according to the Spirit, the things of the Spirit. For the mind set on the flesh is death, but the mind set on the Spirit is life and peace. (Rom. 8:3–6)

One test of a good teacher is how the class behaves if the teacher is called out of the room. Will they obey out of fear of getting caught or out of respect for the teacher and an understanding that it's the right thing to do? The same is true in the military. In a well-trained unit, every soldier knows his role and responsibility. While there are individual soldiers, they are part of a larger unit, company, regiment, brigade, or squadron.

Paul's commands are both personal and corporate. We've been placed in the body of Christ by the saving power of Christ.

We are individually indwelt by the Holy Spirit. He expects us to act according to our new nature. Matt Chandler notes, "This is not an easy walk in our consumer culture in which everything is so polarized. From religion to politics to pop culture, everybody believes that their way is *the* way."[9] How do we live this out? Paul calls us to stand firm. That's a purposeful statement. It's a military term and is used eight times in Paul's writings. We are to stand firm against the world, the flesh, and the devil. We're in a battle. The enemy is doing everything in his power to knock us out of the game. He works to put us on the sidelines or to make us a casualty of war. If you fall, don't give up, get up.

To stand firm means to persevere. We can't afford to budge or be pushed back. We stand for the gospel in the power of the Holy Spirit. We may be different in a multitude of ways, but we are all one in Christ. When Paul calls the church to this kind of consistency, this is not a random thought. Jerry Bridges said, "Endurance and perseverance are qualities we would all like to possess, but we are loath to go through the process that produces them."[10]

In Paul's letters we find similar exhortations:

> . . . walk in a manner worthy of the calling with which you have been called, with all humility and gentleness, with patience, showing tolerance for one another in love, being diligent to preserve the unity of the Spirit in the bond of peace. (Eph. 4:1–3)

> And He gave some as apostles, and some as prophets, and some as evangelists, and some as pastors and teachers, for the equipping of the saints for the work of service, to the building up of the body of Christ; until we all attain to the unity of the faith. (Eph. 4:11–13)

> . . . put on love, which is the perfect bond of unity. Let the peace of Christ rule in your hearts, to which indeed you were called in one body; and be thankful. (Col. 3:14–15)

How are we to stand? In *one spirit* and with *one mind*. This is an unchallengeable message. Paul is being dogmatic about unity as a key to consistency. The enemy is always probing for a crack in the armor, an unlocked door, a window left open. He is searching for ways to expose inconsistency. We must have unity to stand in this battle. One reason people lack purpose is they feel strongly both ways, yet you can't be double-minded and have a singular focus. You can't buy peace by sacrificing truth. Being of one spirit and one mind is the essence of being the body of Christ and a witness to the world.

The idea of the unity of one mind runs throughout the Scriptures.

- The gospel is COMPLETE (Jude 3).
- The gospel is UNIQUE (Col. 1:6–7).
- The gospel is AUTHORITATIVE (1 Cor. 15:1–4).
- The gospel is DYNAMIC (Rom. 1:16).

In the world of social media, everyone has a cause or an agenda. We share, post, and repost things we are passionate about. Unfortunately, the lines get blurry when a post about a new chicken casserole recipe carries the same weight as a post about the impact of immorality on our culture. When Paul calls us to stand firm, he's also calling us to lay aside our personal preferences, agendas, and programs for the good of the gospel.

Standing firm is never easy. However, the consequences of not standing firm can be catastrophic. On the fortieth anniversary of D-Day, President Ronald Reagan stood on the beaches of Normandy and delivered one of the greatest speeches ever given about the cost of freedom. When the Allied forces invaded France on June 6, 1944, it was a defining moment. There was a determination, no matter the cost, to defeat Hitler and Nazi Germany. In remembering that historic day, Reagan said:

> We stand on a lonely, windswept point on the northern shore of France. The air is soft, but forty years ago at this moment, the air was dense with smoke and the cries of men, and the air was filled with the crack of rifle fire and the roar of cannon. At dawn, on the morning of the 6th of June, 1944, 225 Rangers jumped off the British landing craft and ran to the bottom of these cliffs.
>
> Their mission was one of the most difficult and daring of the invasion: to climb these sheer

and desolate cliffs and take out the enemy guns. The Allies had been told that some of the mightiest of these guns were here and they would be trained on the beaches to stop the Allied advance.

The Rangers looked up and saw the enemy soldiers [at] the edge of the cliffs shooting down at them with machine guns and throwing grenades. And the American Rangers began to climb. They shot rope ladders over the face of these cliffs and began to pull themselves up. When one Ranger fell, another would take his place. When one rope was cut, a Ranger would grab another and begin his climb again. They climbed, shot back, and held their footing.

Soon, one by one, the Rangers pulled themselves over the top, and in seizing the firm land at the top of these cliffs, they began to seize back the continent of Europe. Two hundred and twenty-five came here. After two days of fighting, only ninety could still bear arms.

Behind me is a memorial that symbolizes the Ranger daggers that were thrust into the top of these cliffs. And before me are the men who put them there. These are the boys of Pointe du Hoc. These are the men who took the cliffs. These are the champions who helped free a continent. These are the heroes who helped end a war.[11]

If you want to win, you have to fight. If we are going to be salt and light, we have to remember that salt and light are both irritants—salt attacks decay and light attacks darkness. We are soldiers of the light. We must hold our footing. We are called to be New Testament Christians, proclaim New Testament Christianity, and build New Testament churches. We can all say "Amen," but when we actually walk it out, this world system will fight us at every turn. Carnal church members will complain and worldly endeavors will be threatened.

The church in Acts wasn't perfect, but they had a standard we are still trying to duplicate (see Acts 2). I like what Vance Havner wrote: "There is no point spending our time sighing for the church that was. Neither should we settle down in the church that is, satisfied with status quo. We should make our goal the church that ought to be, even though we disturb all who rest at ease in Zion."[12] To consistently stand firm, we must also strive together. To stand firm means taking a defensive position. It is a determination to persevere against the coming onslaught. To strive together is an offensive stance.

Let me apply a sports analogy for a moment. Any good coach will tell you that the key to winning is consistency. Through the years, I've seen too many extremely talented young people who were lazy and inconsistent. You can't take off every other play and be successful. Your playing, living, or serving can't be sporadic. Everyone has an assignment. Some positions and roles may be more glamorous than others, but if the team is to func-tion as a team, they must all consistently do what's expected. The opposing team is committed to stopping you when you're on offense and to running it down your throat when you're on defense. One of the keys in coaching is to teach players to keep their eyes in the right place. If they get distracted, they could be responsible for a blown play. As a believer, the same is true. Keep your eyes on Jesus, don't let anyone or anything distract you from your life assignment.

The difference between a team winning and losing is often in the little things. I was reminded of this while reading my friend Andy Andrews's book, *The Little Things: Why You Really Should Sweat the Small Stuff*. It's the small stuff. The things that the average person misses. The one who excels will see the little things that make a big difference. It's being just one step faster, or releasing the ball just before you get sacked, or knowing how to break a tackle. It looks easy from the cheap seats. That's why in sports (and in church) we've got so many Monday morning quarterbacks. They talk a better game than they live. If you've never done it, don't throw barbs at those who are at least in the arena.

Any team that wants to win plays with passion and pur-pose. Any church that wants to experience healthy growth has passion and purpose. The church must refuse to sit by and watch the culture win. We are in a game where the stakes are life and death, heaven and hell. We can't sit out for one play. God has called us to be faithful. Being faithful is not trying to hold on and maintain our 'holy huddle" until Jesus comes. We need to stand firm in our faith. The devil is trying to knock us off balance. Sometimes we're on offense and sometimes we're on defense. But the clock is ticking and there's work to do.

If you've ever been part of a team, you understand that it's imperative to play as one. There is no "I" or "me" in team. Team players make everyone around them better. The team that Paul traveled with enabled him to do things he couldn't have done otherwise. Imagine what could have been if didn't have a doctor like Luke traveling with him to keep him going. Remember—we are all in this together. Maybe this is what Paul is talking about when he writes to wrestle in company with or to contend with. Paul is calling them to jointly and collectively cooperate and strive together for the advancement of the gospel through a unified church.

Remember, what we believe determines how we behave. If our "it" is that Christ be glorified and the gospel be preached to the nations, then that "it" is a lifelong purpose statement. It will impact our choices and priorities. We are to believe the gospel and behave the gospel. In a time when church attendance is a last-minute decision, we need to decide to follow Jesus, no turning back. In a day when anything and everything can keep people from coming to church, we need to be committed to the local assembly. In a day when we don't want to offend anyone by speaking the truth, we need to speak the truth, in love, without compromise.

These words are not open for discussion or debate. Paul expected the Philippian church to live this way: ". . . whether I come and see you or remain absent" (1:27); "not as in my presence only, but now much more in my absence" (2:12). Paul is saying, "Whether I can always check up on you or not, behave! Live out your faith. Press forward!"

We've put too much faith in programs, personalities, buildings, and methods. Ultimately, what will attract people to Jesus is a purposeful church with a clear commitment to living out the principle of "as He is, so also are we, in this world" (1 John 4:17). What will be most used by God to attract the lost will be when we are adorned with the doctrine of Christ in every aspect. If we do this, there will be setbacks and sometimes suffering. Following Jesus will bring its own unique problems and pressure. Being a Christian is not for sissies. Francis Schaeffer wrote, "We cannot expect the world to believe that the Father sent the Son, that Jesus' claims are true and that Christianity is true, unless the world sees some reality of the oneness of true Christians."[13]

The word *opponents* used in verse 28 is generic in the original Greek and means "whoever they may be." The verb is used of a horse being frightened or spooked. Generally a horse is spooked when it catches something out the corner of its eye. This may sound negative, but it's actually positive. To be unafraid is to be joyfully courageous. Maybe Paul was thinking about the time he and Silas were thrown into the prison in Philippi and they broke out into song. Read verse 27 like this: "Never be frightened, terrified, or a scared person. Regardless of what the circumstances may be, not in a single instance, not in one thing, are you to be frightened by the adversaries, those who lie against, who are hostile, or opponents of the gospel." The key is they are not *your* adversaries; they are adversaries of the gospel. If you are an intentional Christ-follower, you're going to have opponents both inside and outside the church. Don't let fear keep you from being who God saved you to be.

Don't miss this: whether we are talking about standing firm and striving together or contending for the faith, it is ultimately what God will use against His enemies one day to prove the power of the gospel. To know what we face and to face it without fear is in itself a witness. "For to you it has been granted for Christ's sake, not only to believe in Him, but also to suffer for His sake, experiencing the same conflict which you saw in me, and now hear to be in me" (Phil. 1:29–30). The phrase *it has been granted* includes a noun form of grace, meaning, "It has been graced (freely given) to you to suffer for the sake of Christ." We need grace to believe. We need grace to be willing to suffer for what we believe.

The Philippians were fully aware of Paul's sufferings. He had been beaten, imprisoned, and placed in chains. They saw it happen in Philippi, and now they've heard about what was happening in Rome. Why is it that we hear about persecution around the world and see so little of it in America? Because, honestly, we would make lousy martyrs. We are more enthralled by the prosperity gospel than the cross. America has known seasons of revival and awakening. Times in which the Spirit of God was so thick you could cut it with a knife. These were transformational times. Unfortunately, it's been a long time since any move of God like that has swept across our land. I'm praying and believing God for another great move in this land, but it won't happen if we keep parading a caricature of Christianity and calling it the real deal.

The nation of Israel experienced great blessings during the rule of David and Solomon. After them, the nation divided and the end result was tragic. The people of God lost their purpose and fell into idolatry and apostasy. Rehoboam listened to the rash, ungodly advice of his peers and led the nation into idolatry.

> Now Rehoboam the son of Solomon reigned in Judah. Rehoboam was forty-one years old when he became king, and he reigned seventeen years in Jerusalem, the city which the LORD had chosen from all the tribes of Israel to put His name there. And his mother's name was Naamah the Ammonitess. Judah did evil in the sight of the LORD, and they provoked Him to jealousy more than all that their fathers had done, with the sins which they committed. For they also built for themselves high places and sacred pillars and Asherim on every high hill and beneath every luxuriant tree. There were also male cult prostitutes in the land. They did according to all the abominations of the nations which the LORD dispossessed before the sons of Israel. (1 Kings 14:21–24)

The nation was on shaky ground. No longer did they look to God as their source and strength. It wasn't long before

Jerusalem was attacked by Shishak, king of Egypt, who plundered Jerusalem and took away valuable treasures from the Temple. The next verses are key to this story. When you lose your purpose, your life and ministry will be plundered and you'll end up parading a form of godliness with no power.

> He took away the treasures of the house of the LORD and the treasures of the king's house, and he took everything, even taking all the shields of gold which Solomon had made. So King Rehoboam made shields of bronze in their place, and committed them to the care of the commanders of the guard who guarded the doorway of the king's house. Then it happened as often as the king entered the house of the LORD, that the guards would carry them and would bring them back into the guards' room. (1 Kings 14:26–28)

Why point out the gold shields? Vance Havner argues, "they symbolized the prosperity with which God had blessed His people. But Shishak took them, and Rehoboam, to cover his embarrassment, substituted shields of bronze, and everyone must have been reminded of the contrast between his time and the days of Solomon every time they saw the bronze shields."[14]

The church today has allowed the enemy to come in and plunder us. Satan has convinced us that we can't walk in Christ or in the power of the Spirit. We settle for methods and mediocrity, programs and playgrounds, and then try to cover up our defeat by making bronze shields. We wear masks, play games, and look for a faith that doesn't demand too much of us. Just a simple Easter parade, an occasional nod toward God, and we are on our way. In looking back at what happened between the church in Acts 2 and the obvious lack of power as the church moved away from those early days, Harnack writes, "As the proofs of the Spirit and of power subsided after the beginning of the third century, the extraordinary moral tension also became relaxed, paving the way gradually for a morality which was adapted to a worldly life."[15] The church began to compromise, so as to be less offensive to an ungodly age. The result? They become less effective on an ungodly culture.

I personally believe the only hope for us is a revival—God restoring His church to His intent. We need another Martin Luther, John Knox, John Wesley, Charles Spurgeon, Evan Roberts, Hudson Taylor . . . someone, anyone who will state the obvious: "We've substituted shields of bronze for shields of gold." We need men and women of God who can see through the fog and the facade, who can tell the counterfeit from the real. We need people who will not settle for second best. Again, Vance Havner:

> The church is taken up today with much that is
> good, but she is not carrying on in the power of
> Pentecost and there is no use trying to conceal
> the fact that Shishak has substituted his "good"
> for God's best. . . . The world is not deceived:

they know that we have been robbed and all our clever tricks do not deceive. There is no use trying to save our faces. Shishak has taken the shields of gold, our testimony and our power, and we waste time in activities that may help to hide it when our greatest need is to confess it and regain what we have lost.[16]

As I study church history and, in particular, revival history, it is apparent that the people God uses when He chooses to move are people who are purposefully consistent. They are consistent in prayer, consistent in their commitment to the Word of God, passionate about God and the things that matter. They stand firm, strive with other like-minded believers, and leave the results to God.

What if God moved again like He did in 1857? It started in Ireland because of four young men who were persistent and consistent. They began a weekly prayer meeting in a village school, and the following year more prayer meetings started and revival was the common theme of the preachers. The next year, one hundred thousand people were converted in the churches of Ireland in what is marked as the beginning of the Ulster revival of 1859. It was the greatest thing to hit Ireland since the ministry of Saint Patrick. Services were packed with people, there was an abundance of prayer meetings, family prayers increased, Scripture reading was unmatched, Sunday schools prospered, people stood firm, giving increased, vice abated, and crime was reduced significantly.

It's time for us to be the Christians we were saved to be. Then and only then, will the church once again rise up and confront this fallen world with power.

CHAPTER 6

PURPOSEFUL SERVANTS

Philippians 2:1–10

The service that counts is the service that costs.
—Howard Hendricks

JUST HEARING THE word *servant* makes most people cringe. We view it as demeaning. Yet the growth of the kingdom of God is threatened by apathy and a first-world concept of success. We don't see serving as a path to success, but Jesus said the greatest people on the planet are the people who serve. We've sold our souls to the prosperity gospel of privilege, health, wealth and happiness, and the true gospel has suffered. Looking good at all cost has replaced getting on our knees and washing feet.

Charles Lindbergh once said, "It is not the outer grandeur of the Roman but the inner simplicity of the Christian that lived on through the ages."[1] Although Jesus said, "It is more blessed to give than to receive" (Acts 20:35), you won't find a lot of believers signing up for a class on giving. In a world of givers and takers, far too many who claim to be Christ-followers are takers. "What's in it for me?" "What can I get out of it?" The American church has a cancer of narcissism. One need look no further than social media selfies to affirm this truth.

In the Bible, the most common word for a servant is *doulos*, often translated "slave." In Bible times, and even in our history, it's been a term of humiliation. But, if you are a student of Scripture, you'll see that great leaders like Moses, Joshua, David, and the prophets were called servants. In the New Testament, Peter, Paul, James, Jude, and Jesus Himself all wear that title unashamedly. When James and John contended for the best place next to Jesus in eternity, He responded to their arrogant ignorance,

> You know that those who are recognized as rulers of the Gentiles lord it over them; and their great men exercise authority over them. But it is not this way among you, but whoever wishes to become great among you shall be your servant; and whoever wishes to be first among you shall be slave of all. For even the Son of Man did not come to be served, but to serve, and to give His life a ransom for many. (Mark 10:42–45)

For the apostle Paul, Jesus was Lord and Master; Paul viewed himself as nothing more than a servant of his King. As Christ's slave, he was his Lord's witness, missionary, servant, church planter, teacher, preacher, and author. In Barclay's commentary on the Letters of James and Peter, he accurately describes being a servant as becoming "inalienably possessed by God, unqualifiedly at the disposal of God, unquestionably obedient to God and constantly in service to God."[2] If we want to live a life of purpose that pleases God, we have to get on board with the idea of being a servant. Jon Johnston wrote, "Jesus taught them that this world's idea of worth cannot be carried over into his spiritual realm. In Christ's kingdom, there is a complete reversal of earth's values."[3] We see this in Paul's entreaty to the Philippians:

> Therefore if there is any encouragement in Christ, if there is any consolation of love, if there is any fellowship of the Spirit, if any affection and compassion, make my joy complete by

> being of the same mind, maintaining the same
> love, united in spirit, intent on one purpose. Do
> nothing from selfishness or empty conceit, but
> with humility of mind regard one another as
> more important than yourselves; do not merely
> look out for your own personal interests, but
> also for the interests of others. (Phil. 2:1–4)

The word *therefore* is a word that should make us stop and pay attention, as well as look back at the context of what Paul has written previously. In 1:27 he admonished, "Only conduct yourselves in a manner worthy of the gospel of Christ." Paul doesn't tell us what the worthy life is, but he is clear about what it looks like. It is the overflow of a steadfast, consistent life. The result of standing firm, striving together and suffering for the gospel. The overriding desire of Paul for the church was that their lives would match up to the gospel. The consistency of our lives with the life of Christ is a powerful and undeniable witness.

J. A. Motyer notes, "It will convict the world and yourselves also (verse 28), though in different ways! The world it condemns; the church it confirms (verses 29, 30)."[4] The word *only* in 1:27 is repeated in a different way in 2:2: "Make my joy complete." The connecting word *therefore* joining *only* in 1:27 and *make my joy complete* in 2:2 reveals that for Paul, the only way to make his joy complete is by being of the same mind. A united heart and mind with the heart and mind of Jesus. These attitudes are foundational and essential.

Therefore, since there is encouragement in Christ, unity should be our theme as a church. Disunity has destroyed more churches and turned the lost away from the gospel more than anything I can think of. It can rumble under the surface or be a swift undercurrent that sweeps a church down the river of irrelevance. It can be smoldering, and, if left unattended, can start a wildfire that destroys the witness of the people of God. If you've watched the news, when a wildfire breaks out, tragedy, destruction, and death are the end results. Once a forest is burned, the effects are seen for decades to come. The same is true in a divided church. So, why is unity important?

- It's a reflection of the Godhead.
- It's a picture of the Holy Spirit joining people together as one.
- It's the evidence of dying to selfish agendas.
- It's a picture of humility.

John Blanchard writes, "When the Bible speaks about church unity, it speaks of unity not at the expense of truth but on the basis of it."[5] One of Satan's most effective strategies is to convince Christians that being full of themselves is acceptable to God. Unity and service go hand in hand. Paul thought like a pastor. He was concerned for his local church. Nonetheless, he expected them to stand firm in the face of their adversaries and to not complain. Even though he was concerned for their suffering, he called them to count it a privilege if they were called to suffer. And he expected them to have the servant heart of their Master. Only those who think like a servant can follow through on the exhortation to have "one mind, striving together for the faith" (Phil. 1:27).

ENCOURAGEMENT IN CHRIST

The New English Translation phrases 2:1–3 as follows:

> Therefore, if there is any encouragement in Christ, any comfort provided by love, any fellowship in the Spirit, any affection or mercy, complete my joy and be of the same mind, by having the same love, being united in spirit, and having one purpose. Instead of being motivated by selfish ambition or vanity, each of you should, in humility, be moved to treat one another as more important than yourself.

The phrase *encouragement in Christ* can be translated consolation, exhortation, incentive, or comfort. It carries a strong sense of supporting one another. What produces this kind of encouragement? Truth. He then uses the word *comfort* or *consolation*, meaning to call to one's side for comfort and encouragement. It's a love that encourages others to be faithful.

There have been times in all our lives when we know that if not for someone's kind words, encouragement, support, or prayers, we wouldn't have survived. The spiritually sensitive do what a servant would do: they are ready and willing to step in and help. When others are walking out of the room, they are walking in. I see this often as a pastor. When there is a death in a family, our church body steps in immediately. They bring food, clean the house, run errands, go to the cleaners, prepare meals, and sit and listen. These servants lay aside their personal agenda and put away their daily planner to minister to others.

FELLOWSHIP IN THE SPIRIT

Paul continues by talking about our *fellowship* in the Spirit. This refers to our communion, sharing, or participation. The ministry of the Spirit makes us one. This kind of fellowship is not about food; it's from the Spirit and produced by the Spirit. I've heard it said, "Christ supplies grace, God gives love, and the Spirit creates fellowship." When Paul mentions the consolation of love, he is referring to an active, expressive, unhindered love. We often think of being a servant as doing our chores grudgingly, but Paul views being a servant as an act of love.

The seeds of a servant heart will produce visible fruit of the Spirit. In chapter 2, we read, "Make my joy complete by being of the same mind, maintaining the same love, united in spirit, intent on one purpose." Servants have one agenda: to please the Master. We serve the Lord. We serve our family. We serve those who will never appreciate it. The world knows if we are on the same page, and whether we are like-minded. Paul's strategy in chapter 1 is "Christ first," followed by "others next" in chapter 2.

Beginning in verse 3, Paul addresses the bitter seed that will destroy a church or an individual believer—self-centeredness. "Do nothing from selfishness or empty conceit, but with humility of mind regard one another as more important than yourselves; do not merely look out for your own personal interests, but also for the interests of others" (2:3–4). If we aren't living as servants of Christ, if we are selfish and self-centered, word will spread and the gospel witness will be damaged. One way or another, a church's reputation will be known in a community— whether by letter, gossip, email, or word-of-mouth conversations. Social media have magnified the destructive effects of an undisciplined tongue or thumbs typing on a cell phone. Within seconds, you can damage the witness of a person, a church, or, most important, of the gospel, by careless, self-centered words and deeds. That perception quickly becomes reality. If you don't believe me, check out Romans 1:8, 1 Corinthians 5:1, Galatians 1:6–7, and 1 Thessalonians 3:6.

In the nineties, our town of Albany, Georgia, was hit suddenly with a catastrophic five-hundred-year flood. Creeks overflowed their banks, and in some areas the river was nearly fifteen miles wide. Thousands were forced from their homes, and countless businesses, houses, and other properties were destroyed. In the year after the flood, thousands of volunteers from around the country came to our city to help us rebuild. The night the flood hit, we turned our gym into a shelter and had hundreds of people sleeping there for several weeks. Many had nothing more than the clothes on their backs. We served more than twenty thousand meals out of our small church kitchen for the better part of a year. One thing I distinctly remember about that flood was the lack of any sort of racial, ethnic, socioeconomic, or cultural divide. We all had something in common, and we came together as one to help one another. This is the encouragement Paul gives the Philippian church.

Paul warns that we must guard against wrong thinking because it will lead to wrong actions. Wrong thinking makes you selfish. If we are going to have a servant's heart, we have to purposefully evaluate our motives. We cannot afford to have some members of the church thinking they are better than others or assuming they are too good to serve. We can't allow people to think the church is a place where I take and never give back. The gospel is free, but freeloaders don't exhibit New Testament faith.

HUMILITY

Servants are humble people. Humility demonstrates a healthy respect for who God is and who we are because of what God did on our behalf. "Do not think of yourself more highly than you ought, but rather think of yourself with sober judgment. . . . Be devoted to one another in brotherly love. Honor one another above yourselves" (Rom. 12:3, 10 NIV). When Paul writes, "do not merely look out for . . ." in verse 4, he means for his hearers to make their aim greater than self. Don't make it your goal to get things your way, because Jesus didn't look out for His own interests but for yours. Want to test yourself for a servant's heart? Read Romans 15:1–4:

> Now we who are strong ought to bear the weaknesses of those without strength and not just please ourselves. Each of us is to please his neighbor for his good, to his edification. For even Christ did not please Himself; but as it is written, "The reproaches of those who

reproached you fell on me." For whatever was
written in earlier times was written for our
instruction, so that through perseverance and
the encouragement of the Scriptures we might
have hope.

If we are serious about living a purposeful life, we can't be
selective in the Scriptures we quote. In the Beatitudes, Jesus
turned everyone's worldview upside down. The Beatitudes call
us to inside-out living. Jesus embodied these truths and calls
us to do the same as His followers. Think about His life. The
One who held the ruler's scepter took up the servant's basin and
towel. The One who was worshiped by angels laid it all aside
to wash the feet of sinners. Jesus purposefully became a servant
and calls us to be an army of servants.

What Paul is asking of the Philippians is illustrated perfectly in the life of Christ. Jesus was the suffering servant. He
didn't come to be served but to serve. The greatest among us is
the one who serves. God isn't looking for greatness; He's looking for availability. Once I've said, "For me to live is Christ,"
I can't say, "I don't want to serve." Once I confess Jesus as my
Lord and Savior, I cannot sit on the sidelines. Jim Elliot said,
"Wherever you are, be all there. Live to the hilt every situation
you believe to be the will of God." Your life is not your own;
you've been bought with a price. Your life is not for your private
use only. We are here to serve.

One reason we see so much self-centeredness in the church
is we've lost our focus on the purpose of our calling. It's not

enough to be a church attender, go to Bible study, and fill journals with sermon notes—we must do something with all this information and notice the needs of others and apply ourselves to meeting those needs.

There was a lady who was once a member of our church. She was a successful doctor in town who sang in the choir and served faithfully and quietly in various areas of ministry. We lost a true servant when she moved back home to help her mother. I remember one night walking into the Fellowship Center after an event and seeing her wiping down the tables. She had to be at work the next morning before 7:00 a.m., but there she was, doing a menial task. I told her she needed to go home, and she replied, "Oh, pastor, I love doing this." As I think back over her time as a member, everything she did manifested the aroma of Christ. She served, sang, and ministered with the joy of Christ on her face.

The kingdom of God is a kingdom of servants. We stand firm—that's our defensive position. We strive together—that's our offensive position. We serve—that's our witness to the world.

> Have this attitude in yourselves which was also in Christ Jesus, who, although He existed in the form of God, did not regard equality with God a thing to be grasped, but emptied Himself, taking the form of a bond-servant, and being made in the likeness of men. Being found in appearance as a man, He humbled Himself

by becoming obedient to the point of death, even death on a cross. For this reason also, God highly exalted Him, and bestowed on Him the name which is above every name, so that at the name of Jesus every knee will bow, of those who are in heaven and on earth and under the earth, and that every tongue will confess that Jesus Christ is Lord, to the glory of God the Father. (Phil. 2:5–11)

In verse 5, we find a transitional statement. If you want to know what the life of a servant looks like, look to Jesus. He surrendered His rights and came to earth to serve the will of the Father and the needs of man. Paul says we are to have His attitude. The word *have* is present tense, meaning to have and keep on having. We will never find or fulfill our purpose if we think of serving as something we do occasionally or temporarily. Over the course of my ministry, I've watched parents who are willing to serve in the Preschool Ministry when they have preschoolers. Then they are "led" to work with children as their kids get older. Suddenly, they feel "called" to serve students when their kids reach middle and high school. And, not surprisingly, when their kids go off to college, they feel "led" to stop serving and start spending their time and money at the lake, the beach, or the mountains. Their serving was, in essence, selfish. They weren't serving Christ; they were serving their own selfish interests. I'm still waiting on the chapter and verse they use to justify that attitude.

Remember, Paul urged that we do nothing from selfishness or conceit. "Serving" from selfishness and conceit is the opposite of serving because it's in your own best interest to do so. Paul calls us to serve with no thought of the time or cost. This kind of service only comes as a response to being continually aware of the grace shown us by Christ. It means we never push for a position or praise, and there's no thought of "Who will notice?" or "Where's my award for faithful service?" The root of humility is Christ.

Look at the various ways this verse is translated:

- "Treat one another with the same spirit as you experience in Christ Jesus." —Moffatt[6]
- "Have the same attitude that Christ Jesus had." —Goodspeed[7]
- "Let the same disposition be in you which was in Christ Jesus." —Weymouth[8]

Some translate the word *attitude* as "mind." Paul is not talking about our IQ, but rather our disposition. This is about fully cooperating with God's plan and purpose for our lives.

Recently, I went by our local drugstore to pick up some prescriptions and "coincidentally" parked the car and walked inside instead of making my usual trip through the drive-through pickup window. When I got to the counter, there was a lady in line using a cane, so I stepped aside and let her go ahead of me. Two elderly people walked up after her, and I let them go ahead of me too because I wasn't in a rush. I walked around the store for a few minutes and returned to the counter to pick up my prescriptions when I noticed the pharmacist was crying on the phone. When she finished her call I asked her if everything was okay. She said her best friend was dying of cancer, and she was appreciative when I asked if I and our church could be praying for her. Within twenty-four hours, I learned that her friend had passed away. That following Sunday, our church wrote prayer cards to the woman's best friend's husband—now a widower—and I took them to the drug store the next day. It was a simple act, but what if I had been caught up in getting in and out of the store as quickly as possible? I would have missed a ministry moment. How often do we rush through life, missing God-ordained moments to show the love of Jesus by serving and caring for others?

The great conductor Leonard Bernstein was asked, "What's the most difficult instrument to play?" He said, "Second fiddle. I can get plenty of first violinists, but to find one who plays *second* violin with as much enthusiasm or *second* French horn or *second* flute, now that's a problem. And yet if no one plays second, we have no harmony."[9]

Ultimately the choice we make on a daily basis is between serving others and serving self—between playing first and second fiddle. Jesus embodied servant leadership. I'm afraid that too often, the last thing any of us want to be known as is a suffering servant. Everything Jesus did was to serve the purpose and mission for which he was sent. C. Gene Wilkes writes, "We who lead often overlook that the true place of Christlike leadership is out in the crowd rather than up at the head table. Head tables have replaced the towel and washbasin as symbols of leadership among God's people."[10]

One of the major problems in the twenty-first-century church is that we are no longer servants—we are celebrities. We have speakers and singers who sit in green rooms drinking bottled water and picking at a fruit tray until it's their time to hit the stage. We've made our musicians and ministers into rock stars because they have best-selling albums and books and a television ministry. Nothing about the green room reminds me of Jesus. It's the way the world operates; yet it's unacceptable for servants of the Lord to expect or demand (check out the concert rider for your favorite Christian musical group) to be served.

J. Oswald Sanders wrote a classic book on leadership that is a must-read for leaders and laity alike. In *Spiritual Leadership*, he compares natural and spiritual leadership tendencies:

NATURAL	SPIRITUAL
Self-confident	Confident in God
Knows men	Knows God
Makes own decisions	Seeks to find God's will
Ambitious	Self-effacing
Originates own methods	Finds and follows God's methods
Enjoys commanding others	Delights to obey God
Motivated by personal considerations	Motivated by love for God and man
Independent	God-dependent

To quote Gene Wilkes again, "You will never become a servant leader until you first become a servant *to* the leader."

Having served in ministry for more than forty years, I regret to say that much of the leadership I see in the American church is nothing more than natural leadership with a prayer tagged to it for God to "bless our efforts." There is a void of true spiritual leaders in our churches—people who listen to God, learn from God, and speak for God. We are more influenced by the latest *New York Times* best seller than we are by leaders like Moses and Nehemiah. We are more impressed with résumés than righteousness.

Paul had to rebuke more than one church for their attitude. The Corinthians were obsessed with personalities, and they were carnal. God is in the business of honoring those who serve, but the Corinthians thought they were big shots. They even said of Paul, "In person he is unimpressive and his speaking amounts to nothing" (2 Cor. 10:10 NIV). Imagine the arrogance it takes to say that about a man like Paul! But Paul didn't think highly of himself. In fact, he didn't think much of himself at all.

> For Christ did not send me to baptize, but to preach the gospel, not in cleverness of speech, so that the cross of Christ would not be made void. (1 Cor. 1:17)

> If I have to boast, I will boast of what pertains to my weakness. (2 Cor. 11:30)

> And He has said to me, "My grace is sufficient
> for you, for power is perfected in weakness."
> Most gladly, therefore, I will rather boast about
> my weaknesses, so that the power of Christ
> may dwell in me. (2 Cor. 12:9)

The writer of Hebrews reminds us to "lay aside every encumbrance and the sin which so easily entangles us, and let us run with endurance the race that is set before us" (12:1). We often think of those encumbrances and sins as "the really bad stuff" people do. However, the word *encumbrance* refers to anything that would hinder or handicap us as we run this race of faith. *The sin which so easily entangles us* means "in particular, the easily hampering sin."[11] This word phrase is only found in Greek literature and is interpreted as "easy to avoid, easily surrounding, closely clinging to us." The figure is of a runner who, in the Greek games, would run practically naked with every weight discarded.[12] Sin that entangles is the kind of sin that personally trips us up, the places where we are vulnerable because of our temperament or environment, sin that hampers us unless we put it aside.

I believe the number one sin that entangles leaders is the tendency to depend on their own abilities, gifts, talents, education, and experiences, rather than abandoning all of that to surrender to the leadership of the Holy Spirit. While God does use our gifts, abilities, talents, and training, too often we try to add the Holy Spirit to our qualifications rather than walking in the Spirit and leaving our gifts and skills at His disposal. We think we need our abilities to be leaders, but maybe the Holy Spirit is saying, "Lay that aside." In reality, the church is powerless because we can't follow God's purpose for our lives when we are trying to fight the battles in Saul's armor. Until we raise up more leaders like David and stop being impressed with Saul, we will not be used to the max by the Lord Jesus.

The most famous Saul, who became Paul, learned this lesson. He was the Jew of Jews, brilliant, gifted, passionate . . . but it wasn't until he was humbled on the road to Damascus that he became a vessel God could use. When I read Paul's testimony and his letters, I see a man who was bold, but also humble. Paul was strutting on the way to Damascus, but after he met Jesus, he never strutted again.

If we want to be purposeful, we also need to "consider Him who has endured such hostility by sinners against Himself, so that you will not grow weary and lose heart" (Heb. 12:3). According to one study, fifty pastors leave the ministry every day, 365 days a year. It seems many leaders start sending out their résumés at the first sign of trouble. It's time to consider Jesus, who faced hostility but didn't run from it. He is our example, and if we don't follow His lead, we will, in fact, grow weary and lose heart.

The depth of the truth found in the opening verses of Philippians chapter 2 is hard to understand and impossible to explain fully. F. B. Meyer wrote, "This paragraph stands in almost unapproachable and unexampled majesty." Jesus is the ultimate, total, perfect, bodily illustration and demonstration of humility. He humbled Himself, and God has exalted Him.

We don't become God's leaders by exalting ourselves; that's the world's way of leading. What moved Him to lay aside His interests for the interests of others must also motivate us. There are two words to summarize this mind-set: *others* and *obedience*. Jesus humbled Himself and became obedient until death. He was willing to do it. Humility, humbling ourselves, is not a course most of us sign up for, but if we are to live according to God's purpose, we must learn how.

Paul also admonishes, "Do nothing from selfishness." In other words, don't do what you do to be applauded or recognized. This is actually a reference to a church-wide attitude. Don't huddle up in cliques like the elitists in the Empire who think they are better than others!

Please don't misunderstand what I'm about to say. Because of all the recognition our church has received through Sherwood Pictures, we cannot even think about boasting. If we do, we are self-centered and stealing glory that belongs only to God. All we were before the movies and all we've ever been since is a body of believers that surrenders itself to the will of God. We made ourselves available. As the pastor, I've had to remind our congregation that we aren't the greatest thing since sliced bread. We've had people visit our church from more than forty states and several foreign countries who say, "We want to see the church that made the movies." I'm always thinking, "Why? We're just common, everyday folks who surrendered ourselves to the will of God." We aren't celebrities; we're servants. If we allow ourselves to take credit for any of this, we will lose the favor of God. Serving on a movie set doesn't make anyone more spiritual than changing diapers in the nursery for the glory of God.

The purpose of the local church is not to compete with or compare herself to other churches. Our purpose is to humble ourselves and serve the Lord with gladness. No matter what you or your church has done, no one has the right to think more highly of themselves based on their accomplishments or accolades. The only good in us is Jesus. The only pure motive for what we do is glorifying Him, not drawing attention to ourselves. It is imperative that leaders model this for the next generation—loving, serving, and giving as Spirit-filled believers. We need to make sure we're painting the right picture. Paul wanted the church to keep her focus, operate with a biblical worldview, and raise up generation after generation of sold-out servants of the King.

SERVANTS FOR THE LONG HAUL

One of the bittersweet blessings of pastoring a church for nearly thirty years is seeing faithful servants be ushered into the presence of God. Many who were at their prime when I first came to Sherwood are now reaching the stage of life where they just can't physically do what they used to do. I have been blessed to serve alongside men and women who have taught preschoolers for thirty and forty years, others who have been ushers, greeters, and teachers for decades. They didn't bounce around from one ministry to another; rather, they planted their lives in a ministry, fulfilling God's purpose for their lives. They feel called to serve in a particular area and they give themselves to it without reservation or hesitation. The reason we have a leadership crisis in the American church today is lack of purpose. People serve when it's convenient, and they want to be applauded and recognized for what they do. We need to go back to the biblical paradigm of saints who serve faithfully as long as God gives them breath.

If you want to live a life on purpose, you can't "feel led" to take a break every year or two. Any leader will tell you that the world is run by tired men and women. We all get tired, but we are not to grow weary in well doing. Serving the Lord is not a two-year enlistment program; it's a lifelong commitment. If we fail to be purposeful leaders, we are going to create churches that will not stand the test of time. Paul wanted to ensure that, as the church began to grow and mature, they kept the basics in focus. Here's the all-too-common pattern: the first generation has convictions because they experienced powerful deliverance and salvation. The second generation has beliefs, but they often act out of rote responsibility and take blessings for granted because they weren't eyewitnesses to the powerful work. They forget that someone paid the price before them, and the sin of ingratitude begins to set in. Eventually instead of humble service, the mind-set is, "What's in it for me?" The third generation has seen the compromised lives of their parents who lived with less conviction and more opinion. Therefore, their belief system is watered-down, their faith is spotty, and their service is sporadic at best. By the fourth generation, the real danger is apostasy—walking away from the New Testament faith altogether.

How can we stay purposeful? The example is in our servant Savior. He is our source and supply. Paul holds high our Lord and says, "Look to Him. Be like Him." One commentator said trying to explain these verses about Christ is like sending an assistant to a do-it-yourself store and asking him to paint the ceiling of the Sistine Chapel.

These words in Philippians 2 were used by the early church as a hymn of praise. When I read these words I have to ask, "Have I emptied myself of self? Am I daily dying to self? Am I purposefully taking up the cross?" As many theologians through the years have noted, Jesus voluntarily laid down the independent exercise of His divine attributes. He didn't give up His deity; He laid aside the glories of His deity.

> . . . although He existed in the form of God, [He] did not regard equality with God a thing to be grasped, but emptied Himself, taking the form of a bond-servant, and being made in the likeness of men. Being found in appearance as a man, He humbled Himself by becoming obedient to the point of death, even death on a cross. For this reason also, God highly exalted Him, and bestowed on Him the name which is above every name, so that at the name of Jesus every knee will bow, of those who are in heaven and on earth and under the earth, and that every tongue will confess that Jesus Christ is Lord, to the glory of God the Father. (Phil. 2:6–11)

In these verses we see:

- Christ's selfless action (v. 6)
- Christ's servant heart (v. 7)
- Christ's sacrificial offering (v. 8)
- Christ's glorious exaltation (vv. 9–11)

The Sovereign is a Servant and the Servant is Sovereign. The word *exalted* in verse 9 is used only here in the New Testament, and it means "to lift above or beyond; to hyper exalt; to exalt to supremacy of the highest order." Jesus has been given the highest possible name. Why? He redeemed man. God's only Son is God's only way to salvation. He is the central figure of time and eternity and the center of all true worship. Three times in three verses the word *every* appears. This speaks not to universal salvation but to universal subjugation. We serve a Savior who became a servant so that we might serve the rest of our life for His glory. A man asked a rabbi, "Why in the olden days would God show Himself to people, but today nobody ever sees God?" The rabbi answered, "Because nowadays nobody can bow low enough."

We need to humble ourselves if we are going to fulfill God's purpose for our lives. Before we leave this passage and move on to the next chapter, let me challenge you. As you look around, is your church more like the Corinthian church or the Philippian church? Paul had to cut the Corinthians down to size. They were arrogant on multiple levels—a far cry from the example of Christ. If the apostle Paul were to show up at your church, would his sermon text for the day be a rebuke or an encouragement? Would he have to address the carnality of the leadership, or would he applaud the servant spirit? I wonder what the message would be to the average church from most of our biblical heroes? Would they applaud our laser focus or would they rebuke us for the rabbit trails we constantly chase? Would they find in us humility, gentleness, kindness, and a servant heart? Or would they assume our church vision statement is "It's all about me!" Do we fully embrace the idea that God has "chosen the foolish things of the world to confound the wise" (1 Cor. 1:27 KJV) as a statement of purpose for servants?

Gayle D. Erwin calls the Lord's disciples "a motley crew." He says of Christ's followers:

> Jesus went to the streets and wharves and picked out the strangest crew ever to be sent out on a mission to change the world. Had you been walking within fifty feet of them you probably would have detected the odor of fish. . . . Some of them had heavily identified accents inappropriate to the need for eloquence on the team. He was found constantly among the sordid—from the violent to the crafty to the sensual.[13]

This motley crew became world changers. Cities were impacted and empires were altered because God chose a rag-tag group the world never would have picked. I believe God used the disciples to be servant leaders because they had first learned to serve the Lord. If you want to lead, you first have to learn to follow. Let's face it—if we are too good to serve, we are of no use for the kingdom of God.

When I was growing up, we often sang the old hymn "Wherever He Leads, I'll Go" during the invitation. We need to get back to that kind of thinking. If we do, when we do, we will have the attitude of Christ and a self-centered world will take note of it.

CHAPTER 7

LIVING ON PURPOSE
IS PRACTICAL
Philippians 2:12–3:7

All who are ignorant of the purpose for which
they live are fools and madmen.
—John Calvin

Christianity is nothing less and can be nothing
more than relationship to Christ.
—W. H. Griffith Thomas

PREVIOUSLY PAUL HAD been pleading for self-renunciation and humility. He has pictured Jesus as our pattern, and now he dives into the process of all this becoming a reality. If you are going through such a process, you are either learning something new or reminding yourself of truths, principles, and practices you know but aren't living up to at the highest level. At some point, we have to learn to stand on our own. While we need the body of Christ, in the end, no one can be disciplined for us. Paul knew he would one day pass off the scene, and it was important that these believers learn to stand for Christ without his help.

I've had several people in my life that I have leaned on heavily for advice, wisdom, counsel, and insight. The first was Vance Havner. When I was a young man, I devoured his books, exchanged letters with him, and saw him every chance I could get. I still remember the phone call telling me he had died. Suddenly the man who influenced my ministry more than any other was gone.

At about the same time, God brought Ron Dunn into my life. I first heard Ron preach shortly after he buried his oldest son. A few years later, we began to develop a relationship that was as dear to me as any I've ever had. Ron taught me to be myself, to dig deeper to find the truth in the Word, and to trust God in difficult times. Ron had health problems the last few years of his life, but I never anticipated that God would take him when He did. I was driving down the interstate in Atlanta taking Warren and Betty Wiersbe to the airport when my phone rang. It was Joanne, Ron's long-time assistant, and she simply said, "Michael, he's gone." The rest of that day is still a fog. I couldn't believe it. Ron was a friend, a hero, a mentor. He had preached a Bible Conference for me for sixteen con-secutive years. Not a day goes by that I don't miss him.

PREPARED TO STAND IN THE REAL WORLD

One day the Philippian church got the news that Paul had been executed. He was trying to prepare them for that day. He didn't want them to stumble and falter in their faith. He had started a good work in them years before, and he wanted them to continue on "now much more in my absence."

Purposeful people live in the real world. They know it's not fair. They know life will throw you a curve when you least expect it. Therefore, they learn to live by faith. They under-stand that life goes on even when it seems the whole world has come to an end. If you're going to be purposeful, you've got to find out why God placed you here. Too many people waste their lives trying to be someone else. Rather than imitators of Christ, we imitate someone we admire. Rather than following the life of Christ as the pattern of our life, we pattern ourselves after some celebrity or a person we look up to. In the end, we become caricatures or copycats of someone else, not the person God saved us to be.

To be honest, I did that to some extent with Vance Havner and Ron Dunn. I lived off their faith, their ministries, their books. There were times when my faith was second-hand. When they passed away, the reality hit me that there would be no more phone calls, letters, visits, or new sermons. The choice now was to act on what I had been taught and live it out daily. Left to ourselves, we won't grow up. Far too many in the family of faith are living a second-hand faith. In opting to lean totally on others, hoping their faith and prayers will see us through, we fail to become fully devoted followers of Jesus.

Paul wanted these believers to know that sooner or later, they would have to stand on their own. Alistair Begg communicated, "Moralism says to unbelievers, 'Be what you are not.' Christianity says to believers, 'Be what you are.'"[1] Paul commanded them to work out what he's been talking about. He jumps right out of this incredible passage on the exaltation of Christ and gets very practical. He begins verse 12 with *so then* or *therefore*. "In light of what I've said about Jesus, here's how you need to behave. This is the direction for your daily decision making."

We all have to figure this out. The reality is, one day, things are going to change. If you don't grow up now, you may never grow up. One day:

- Paul will be gone ("much more in my absence . . .").
- Your hero will die.
- Your mentor will no longer be there.
- Your parents or grandparents won't be there for you to lean on.
- You'll move away and no one will make you go to church.
- You'll get married and have to figure out this whole Christian marriage thing.

- You'll have to stop depending on who is preaching on a particular Sunday to determine whether or not you'll go to church.

Even before these realities hit, you have to decide what you believe and why you believe it. Every believer has to embrace these words of Paul if they are ever going to make substantial gains in their spiritual development. The sooner a person learns this truth, the better off they will be.

> So then, my beloved, just as you have always obeyed, not as in my presence only, but now much more in my absence, work out your salvation with fear and trembling; for it is God who is at work in you, both to will and to work for His good pleasure. Do all things without grumbling or disputing; so that you will prove yourselves to be blameless and innocent, children of God above reproach in the midst of a crooked and perverse generation, among whom you appear as lights in the world, holding fast the word of life, so that in the day of Christ I will have reason to glory because I did not run in vain nor toil in vain. (Phil. 2:12–16)

WORK OUT YOUR SALVATION

We know that salvation is by grace through faith. We cannot work our way to God. We know it's a gift of God, lest any of us think about boasting. But Paul commands his readers to work out their salvation. In Ephesians 2:10 he writes, "We are His workmanship, created in Christ Jesus for good works, which God prepared beforehand so that we would walk in them." Grace leads to works that are a testimony of the grace we've received. Lehman Strauss wrote, "God nowhere is said to call upon an unsaved person to work out a salvation that He has not worked in, but He fully expects the inwrought work of regeneration to be worked out by the regenerated one."[2] The verb *to work out* demands constant energy and effort. In light of all that God has done for us, we need to work out what He's worked into us.

The word *salvation* in the Latin root is a word for a salve or ointment used for healing. We were saved to be made whole. The Greek word is *soteria*, meaning not only salvation but also preservation. The very word implies the doctrine of eternal security. What God saves, He doesn't lose. But that does not mean, in any way, that we can make excuses or put our lives in neutral until we glide into the pearly gates. What are we to do with our salvation? Grow up. Be mature. Work. Produce. Commit. Accomplish. We are to cultivate our salvation to the point of maturity and bearing fruit. The idea is that we are to keep on working it out until its fulfillment. There is also the idea of perseverance. We are to work at it and stay at it.

Paul is calling on the whole church to work out what God has worked in them. We will never work out our salvation if all we do is wait for some magical experience that transforms us overnight from a caterpillar into a butterfly. To put it another way, Guy King wrote, "I am to mine what is already mine."[3] I am to work humbly every day to get the nuggets of grace to the surface. There was an old saying among miners: "There's gold in them there hills." Well, in you are found the riches of being in Christ, but you have to dig deep and develop them. This is a call to practical obedience. The Philippians were to do this immediately and consistently. Because Jesus is our model for submission and obedience, Paul expected the believers to submit and obey. As children of God, we are not saved only to go into a holding pattern. He didn't instruct them to work for it or at it, but to work it out. Express your salvation in tangible ways. Show what the life of Christ looks like manifest in the life of a believer.

The phrase *with fear and trembling* indicates an obedient response of turning away from that which would dishonor Christ. Grace is free, but it's not cheap. We must take our salvation seriously. There should be a healthy fear of living or acting in a way that grieves the Spirit. We should be conscious each day that Christ is not a *part* of my life, He *is* my life. Without Him, I am nothing. All of us are aware of how easy it is to stumble or fall into temptation. This warning is a reminder that God expects obedience, not to be saved but because we have been saved. The minute I think I'm exempt, I become a target for the world, my own flesh, and the devil.

There is no room for flippancy in the life of the believer. It's inexcusable if we are disciplined in our diet and exercise but casual and indifferent in our spiritual development. We are to have a "sense of awe and respect." What is lacking in many believers today is a sense of reverential awe. We desire enter-tainment more than exposition. We demand a miracle a day to keep the devil away. We want the pastor and staff to do our Christian living for us. We expect others to serve so we can get a free ride. Those attitudes reveal a total lack of reverential awe of God. It's a flippancy that should not be condoned but condemned. Why? The flesh will always win with that attitude. Lehman Strauss noted, "We need to fear the flesh since it is weak and will fail us every time. We need to fear the world because it is ready to let loose its criticism of our failures. We need to fear Satan because he is ever seeking to break down our resistance that we might fall into temptation."[4] God is able, but we are responsible. God worked in the past, and He is working in the present. We are to cooperate so that we don't become another statistic.

"It is God who is at work in you, both to will and to work for *His* good pleasure" (Phil. 2:13, emphasis mine). How often do we acknowledge and appropriate this truth? It is God who energizes and empowers us. It's the work of the Holy Spirit. As we walk in fellowship with God, we walk in His power. The same Holy Spirit who empowered Peter's work with the Jews and Paul's work to reach the Gentiles also empowers us. Grace doesn't make us lazy, nor does it get us out of the work we've been called to do. "But by the grace of God I am what I am, and His grace toward me did not prove vain; but I labored even more than all of them, yet not I, but the grace of God with me" (1 Cor. 15:10). Peter was primarily called to the Jews, and Paul was primarily called to the Gentiles, but both required God to energize and enable them.

God works out what He has worked in. The phrase *to will and to work* means God works in us both the willing and the working. Paul is dealing with the visible results of the inner working of the Spirit—the divine dynamic or the power to live up to His commands and expectations. God's demands are backed by God's power. Every command is backed by a promise. Paul wrote to the Thessalonians, "Faithful is He who calls you, and He also will bring it to pass" (1 Thess. 5:24). We should pray, "Lord, You can demand whatever You want of me as long as You provide what I need to meet that demand." As God is working, we are cooperating with Him in the work. And we are working "for His good pleasure." It pleases God when we cooperate, yield, abide, and walk in fullness. Living to please God is no small thing.

One preacher said it this way: "Think of Philippians 2:13 as our practice and then what Paul says in Ephesians 1:5 as our position in Christ and Ephesians 1:9 as God's purpose." This is not rocket science. It's living out the life of Christ in the daily grind!

Next, Paul admonishes the Philippians, "Do all things without grumbling or disputing" (2:14). It's clearly a call to contentment and a command that is all-inclusive. God's people who are purposeful in their walk will not be guilty of complaining, murmuring, and whining. If you know a troublemaker in a church, it's a sure sign they aren't obeying these commands. If the church is arguing, fussing, fighting, or even headed toward a split, you'll find within her ranks that whiners have too much control. To complain is to have the undertones of dissatisfaction.

Sadly, you don't have to look far to discover this crippling disease in the body of Christ. People whine about God's work and God's will. They question the will of God and cripple the work of God. You find rumblings of discontentment. Those who aren't working out their salvation will begin to develop the attitude that God is the one who needs to compromise so they can live as they please. Complaining will lead to disputing. The use of these words together indicates these thoughts and actions are not so much against God as against other believers. Paul will address this when he names the two women who can't get along later in the book. Disputing refers to thoughts that are not only evil, but also doubtful. Thoughts eventually work themselves out in deeds.

I served a few troubled churches early in my ministry. Their influence was null and void with the lost in the community. They thought quarreling, fussing, gossip, dissension, and rebellion against authority were acceptable in the church. Here's where they missed the whole point: you can't find one instance in the Bible where God or God's man ever ignored murmuring, grumbling, or complaining. God hates it, and He will deal with it. It's not Christlike; it's worldly and divisive. The reason churches are dying and young people are rejecting the church as an institution is not because it's no longer valid. It's simply the reaction to seeing God's people acting like the devil.

Remember, this is a letter to a local church. Paul wants them to work on keeping these kinds of attitudes out of the fellowship.

In my first full-time church job as a youth pastor, we had monthly business meetings. Going to those meetings was like having a root canal with no anesthesia. There was one man who I remember in particular—everyone in the church talked about how he prayed such beautiful prayers. He did . . . but at a business meeting, he was full of the devil. He must have had a Ph.D. in character assassination. Over the course of my two years on that staff, we lost dozens of students who were new Christians but became disillusioned by the carnality of many church members.

After Paul has pointed out what not to do, he turns to another positive command. This is a call to consistency: ". . . so that you will prove yourselves to be blameless and innocent, children of God above reproach in the midst of a crooked and perverse generation, among whom you appear as lights in the world" (2:15). These words tell us how to recognize real believers in this world. They are blameless, innocent, and above reproach, and they shine like lights. There can be little doubt that our purpose is to stand out in this crooked world. Blamelessness has to do with our outward condition. From the world's perspective, our lives should not be used as an example of hypocrisy. Our lives are to be above reproach. The word *innocent* has to do with our inward condition. It's the same word used in Matthew 10:16 ("harmless as doves" KJV). A good way to translate it is "pure and innocent." Our thoughts and motives should be without guile. We act out of a pure heart. As God examines my life, there is nothing that will keep Him from using me.

The call is to be "above reproach"—no blemishes or defects. We are ambassadors, representatives of Jesus in a crooked and perverse generation. The word *crooked* deals with something unscrupulous or dishonest. Lacking integrity. One who can't be trusted. To be *perverse* is to turn away or distort. As believers, we've been empowered to "appear as lights in the world." In this dark world, we are called to shine.

- We've been delivered from the power of darkness (Col. 1:13).
- We walk in the light (1 John 1:7).
- We should reflect Christ who is "the Light of the world" (John 9:5).

All of us know people who live like a light in a dark world. Their lives just brighten a room when they walk in. Not long ago, one of those lights at our church went to heaven. We all called her Miss Christine. She passed away on her ninety-forth birthday. Christine was the happiest, most content, positive woman I believe I've ever met. Probably twenty years ago, I went to see her in the hospital and didn't think she would get out or that I would ever see her again. She proved me and the doctors wrong. On Sundays you could see Miss Christine, who was short and could have been blown over by a good breeze, standing and raising her hands in worship. Even in her eighties and nineties, she absolutely loved praise and worship. She told people about Jesus. She loved life and lived it to the fullest.

When my wife and I went to see her in the hospital a few days before she died, she was very weak and ready to meet Jesus. She said to me, "Many years ago my husband died, and that day Jesus became my husband and He has met every need of my life." Just knowing those few facts about her, you'll understand why we all wanted to grow up and be like Miss Christine. When you get to heaven, you might want to look her up. She'll be the petite little lady with her hands in the air dancing before the throne.

Who do you want to be like? What characteristics do you want to be evident in your life? Let me encourage you to read the biographies of great men and women of faith. Find out why they were used by God. None of them were perfect, but they were available. One of the long-time associates of Dr. Billy Graham was Grady Wilson. Grady once said, "God is using Billy Graham because He has found a man that He can trust."

I love what F. B. Meyer said when he was eighty-two years old: "I have but one great ambition in life—that is to be an errand boy for Jesus Christ." We are called to place ourselves at God's disposal. There's not a lot written about the two men Paul mentions at this point, but they were important enough to have their names in the Word of God. Paul mentions Timothy and Epaphroditus. Timothy is mentioned twenty times in the New Testament. He was a faithful servant and minister. Epaphroditus was simply a messenger, but his name will stand for all eternity because Paul saw in him the life of Christ. What characterized them? For one thing, they were obviously willing to serve others. They gave of themselves so the ministry could go forward. These two brought joy to Paul's life. Their purpose was to serve the church and to serve the apostle. Timothy had a kindred spirit; he was like-minded with Paul. He served Paul like a child serving his father. Epaphroditus was called a brother, fellow worker, fellow soldier, and messenger. That's quite a testimony of his value to Paul. Paul instructs the church in how they should treat these men. They were to be received with all joy and held in high regard. Why? They had earned it, and they deserved it. These men were selfless servants.

If you want to be talked about fondly, live out the purpose of God for your life. Please God, and the true church will receive you with joy and hold you in high regard. Let me ask, do you receive the people God sends your way with joy? Would they say it was a joy to be around you? Is your church full of joy or would a visiting preacher shake the dust off his feet the minute he got out the door? Joy is one of the ways we show the world the light. You may live or work in a dark place, but you can have joy. Missionaries throughout the ages have been sent to dark places, but the joy of serving God has turned a desert or a jungle into paradise. God entrusts faithful, joyful people with a servant's heart to these kinds of places.

PURPOSEFUL ABOUT JOY

In the midst of a crooked and perverse world, it's hard to have joy. In fact, you won't have joy if you are waiting for a feeling instead of claiming the power of the Spirit within you. In a dark place, a light can bring great joy. When the power goes out, there is some level of joy when you find a flashlight or a candle. Jesus is the light of the world, and He told us to be the same. Like the moon, we have no light of our own. We are reflecting the light of the life of Christ. The Bible talks about joy too much for us to ignore it or pretend it's not essential. Joy is a key word in the faith—the birthright of believers. It is a supernatural exhilaration in God and His grace.

"These things I have spoken to you, that My joy may be in you, and that your joy may be made full" (John 15:11). Joy is not about happiness. Happiness is beyond our happenings and control. I know this—there is no delight in seeing a shallow Christian or a brother or sister in Christ who has been deceived or a believer who is stagnant or stalled out in their spiritual journey. But there is great delight in doing the will of God.

Paul talks about rejoicing and sharing one another's joy. He's not making a suggestion; he's stating a command. No matter what happens, we should all have joy as a core value. Joy and rejoicing are not optional responses for believers. "Rejoice always; pray without ceasing; in everything give thanks; for this is God's will for you in Christ Jesus. Do not quench the Spirit" (1 Thess. 5:16–19). Would you agree that too many twenty-first-century saints have unbiblical responses to crises, problems, and adversity? False teaching about our happiness and well-being has left us spiritually impoverished. We've bought the lie that God's purpose is to make us healthy, wealthy, and wise. Paul wants the church to be prepared for the coming persecution. It's time those of us who live in the land of the free and home of the brave wake up to the fact that persecution is coming.

Do you check out when you hear a sermon you've heard before? Or when you hear a sermon from a familiar text? Does your mind wander? Do you think, *Oh, I've heard this. I know all about this*, and then start thinking about your to-do list for the week? Paul tells us we need repetition. "To write the same things again is no trouble to me, and it is a safeguard for you" (Phil. 3:1). Paul is about to warn them about phonies, imposters, and charlatans who could rob them of their joy in the Lord. He says, "I know I'm repeating myself, but I don't mind it . . . and you need to be reminded of these things."

After nearly thirty years of pastoring the same church, I've preached nearly two thousand sermons at Sherwood. That number doesn't include devotions, weddings, funerals, outside speaking, blogs, or books. At times I will repeat a quote or a story I've shared before. It's not because I don't work to stay fresh. I do it because the truth is the same, but the crowd is different, and because, if we are growing, we hear it differently than the first time we heard it. A great danger for pastors, leaders, and writers is the desire for novelty. We want to be cute and cutting edge. If we aren't careful, we will ignore the basics (the foundational truths) and build a church on sand. The question is never, "Have you heard that truth before?" The question is, "Are you acting on it? Are you applying it?" The reason many aren't happy in the Lord is they are trying to find fulfillment in novelty. They want cake and ice cream, but they don't want the meat of the Word. Ultimately they start chasing every fad, a new church, a new preacher, a new podcast, the latest conference, or the best-selling book and are never grounded. They know a lot about what the Word says, but they aren't applying it to their lives. We rejoice in Christ and Christ alone. The key to a purposeful life is obedience. Failing to obey God and work out your salvation with fear and trembling will ultimately lead you down the road of chasing novelty, and you will be left vulnerable to false teachers and deceptive teachings.

Paul now turns to a serious warning of danger lurking in the shadows:

> Beware of the dogs, beware of the evil workers, beware of the false circumcision; for we are the true circumcision, who worship in the Spirit of God and glory in Christ Jesus and put no confidence in the flesh, although I myself might have confidence even in the flesh. If anyone else has a mind to put confidence in the flesh, I far more: circumcised the eighth day, of the nation of Israel, of the tribe of Benjamin, a Hebrew of Hebrews; as to the Law, a Pharisee; as to zeal, a persecutor of the church; as to the righteousness which is in the Law, found blameless. But whatever things were gain to me, those things I have counted as loss for the sake of Christ. (Phil. 3:2–7)

Paul is speaking of the Judaizers who were trying to steal the church's joy. Paul carefully chooses his terms, not as derogatory comments, but as clear pictures of the present danger.

An honest Bible teacher will not only declare the truth of the Word, but he will also expose the error of false teachers.

The church militant can easily become the church decadent and the church complacent. The Judaizers hounded and harassed Paul his entire ministry. They taught that to come to Christ a person had to become a Jew first. They followed Paul around constantly, contradicting the gospel and confusing the church. The three warnings Paul gives here are a reminder that the world, flesh, devil, and false teachers will do everything in their power to keep you from living out God's purpose for your life. First, beware of the dogs who prowl streets in packs, snapping, snarling, and attacking others. These dogs were perverting the gospel and tearing its message apart.

We don't have much trouble with Judaizers today, but we do have people who want to break fellowship over secondary issues or doctrines—thus adding to the gospel, just as the Judaizers added to the gospel. Many want to argue over their preferences regarding the doctrine of salvation, yet they never win the lost. Most of the theological discussions I hear between the various camps regarding salvation sound like a bunch of beggars arguing over a wallet, and all of them are broke.

Paul would say that these dogs parade preferences over convictions. Our churches are full of people who go to the First Baptist Church of Preference. They would rather argue over which translation we use or whether we have hymns or choruses than fulfill the Great Commission. Their vision statement is, "Let the world go to hell; we have a church just like we want it."

For the Jews, *dogs* had a distinct meaning. Jews referred to Gentiles as dogs—those outside the covenant, the unclean. Don't miss the point: Paul is saying these Judaizers were the unclean dogs outside the covenant. He goes on to call them evil workers, the kind of folks who never miss a chance to stir things up. They major on minors, they make issues out of non-issues, and they value opinions over the Word.

G. K. Chesterton wrote, "People think that when they do not believe in God they believe in nothing, but the fact is they will believe in anything."[5] These kind of evil workers worm their way into a fellowship in a thousand ways to get the church off track, teaching a works-based salvation. These people thought they were doing God's work, but Paul says they were evil and their teachings led to the works of the flesh. F. B. Meyer says they are fanatical and unbalanced. They are the cranks of the church; they introduce fads, exaggerate the importance of trifles, catch up on every new theory and follow it to the detriment of truth and love. "It is impossible to exaggerate the harm these people do."[6] The subtle danger of all of this is, if you listen to them and follow their teachings, it will make it easier for the church to "get along and go along" with the pagan Roman Empire. The stark contrast of the life of Christ brings attention that dead religion will never bring. Rome considered Judaism a legal religion, but Christianity was a mystery to them.

BOASTING IN JESUS

Paul continues by warning of the false circumcision. These were the flesh mutilators, referring to pagan rituals. They were slaves to external signs, rules, and standards and were more concerned about outward ordinances than inward righteousness. These men mutilated the gospel of grace—literally, they were butchers who left a bloody path everywhere they went. This is a scathing description. When a religious practice loses its true meaning, it becomes a pagan practice. "Some men came down from Judea and began teaching the brethren, 'Unless you are circumcised according to the custom of Moses, you cannot be saved'" (Acts 15:1). Circumcision was a sign and seal of the covenant with Abraham. The Judaizers were no different than the Pharisees. They had rules and regulations and were proud of their outward acts . . . but they had not circumcised their hearts. The symbol had no spiritual reality. Yesterday's Judaism is today's legalism.

Here we find a biblical course correction that was needed to keep the church focused. We are the true circumcision. We are to use the knife on our heart, not our flesh. Let the Holy Spirit take control and deal with your heart so you'll walk in the Spirit and not take the detour of outward religion with no power. Paul gives us an indication of what real believers do. They purposefully "worship in the Spirit of God and glory in Christ Jesus and put no confidence in the flesh." This is not just about an attitude, but a way of life. Sometimes I wonder how that early church changed the world. After all, they didn't have religious television, radio, podcasts, websites, sermon CDs or MP3s, seminars, conferences, or camps. I'm amazed at all we have now, and yet we make nowhere close to the impact they made. What they did have was Jesus. We boast in our stuff; Paul specifically tells us to boast about Jesus.

Previously Paul has used others as illustrations of Christian living, but now he uses his own life as an example. The apostle lists his qualifications, and his résumé was quite impressive from a worldly point of view. One of the greatest statements I ever heard was from Vance Havner: "Our efficiency without God's sufficiency is only a deficiency." Paul would have written "Worthless" over all his religious accomplishments prior to knowing Christ. He was a Jew by birth, a Greek by speech, a Roman by citizenship, a lawyer by training, a tentmaker by trade, and an apostle by the grace of God. Yet he counted all this as loss compared to knowing Christ. As Vance Havner said, "The work of God cannot be done in the energy of the flesh. Too much religious activity is just old Adam in his Sunday clothes."[7]

The word *flesh* is used different ways in the New Testament. Here it means several specific things:

1. *We can have pride in our religious heritage.* We know this tendency. "I was born a Baptist." "My grandfather was a preacher."
2. *We can have pride in our intellect or position.* It is possible to be a walking encyclopedia of Bible knowledge and know all the answers without knowing Christ as *the* answer.
3. *We can have pride in our accomplishments.* How many of us have doctored our résumé to sound more impressive?

Paul didn't have to doctor his résumé. Paul would say, "If you want to know who has a right to boast, I do. But of all the things I thought were so important, I've written them off. All the things that I accomplished before I met Christ are worthless."

Paul specifically listed his accomplishments so that he could write them off as worthless compared to Christ. But look how closely we list the same accomplishments in order to prop up our own sense of worth:

"Circumcised the eighth day"	"I was baptized at age nine"
"Nation of Israel"	"I was born in a Christian country"
"Tribe of Benjamin"	"I'm a Southern Baptist"
"Hebrew of Hebrews"	"I was born to Christian parents"
"Pharisee"	"I don't smoke, and I don't chew, and I don't go with girls who do"
"Persecutor of church"	"I point out the people I don't agree with"
"Blameless"	"I was selected Man of the Year. I achieved my Perfect Attendance pin in Sunday school"

But Paul stops and puts this into plain and simple words that anyone can understand: "But whatever things were gain to me, those things I have counted as loss for the sake of Christ. More than that, I count all things to be loss in view of the surpassing value of knowing Christ Jesus my Lord, for whom I have suffered the loss of all things, and count them but rubbish so that I may gain Christ" (3:7–8). The word *loss* there is not a pretty or soft word. It is the word for dung—it's worthless.

What is the test of a valid experience? Simply put, does it bring me into a deeper knowledge and love for Jesus? It's not just knowing about Him; it's knowing Him. There's an intimacy with Christ. Paul's ambition was to know Christ, no matter what that involved. Knowing Christ wasn't a free pass to avoid suffering; in fact, it led to suffering. Jesus wasn't an added activity or the key to success. He was Paul's life. Abraham was a friend of God. Moses spoke to God face-to-face. Paul knew Christ. The blood of Jesus and the resurrection had released Paul from all guilt and shame. Sam Gordon said, "This is not the know of intellect, but the know of intimacy."[8] That didn't mean that Paul got a pass from "dangers, toils, and snares." He had enemies who fought against him everywhere he went, and he identified with Christ in "the fellowship of his sufferings." We want the power of the resurrection without the fellowship of suffering. In hell's game plan, sleeping saints are allowed to go undisturbed. But once awakened, they are targets. Joe Stowell writes, "The distance between knowing him and knowing about him is vast. And the space between these two experiences separates the spectators from intimate participants."[9]

To be "conformed to His death" (3:10) reminds us that Paul has moved in this one verse from resurrection to suffering to death. On the surface it looks like he needs to change the order, but in truth, we can't have a resurrection without a death. To be conformed to His death is to die to self daily—daily reckoning of self to be crucified with Christ. Temptations don't appeal to a dead man. The world, the flesh, and the devil don't have any allure. Fame, fortune, power, or pleasure can no longer tug at the heart. Paul clearly wants us to understand that he possesses an undeniable desire and an unhindered purpose.

In his book *Faithful Unto Death: Fifteen Young People Who Were Not Afraid to Die for Their Faith*, Myron Augsburger tells the story of sixteenth-century young people who lived out these truths. One in particular, Gerrit Cornelis Boon, who died in 1571, got my attention. Gerrit was a young boatman in Amsterdam. After hearing the Word of God, Gerrit was saved and became a member of the Anabaptist brotherhood. During this time, hundreds of Anabaptists were arrested and executed. Gerrit knew that making this commitment to Christ could lead to his arrest and even death. As a boatman he had heard many stories as he carried people to their destinations. In June of 1571 he tied his boat to the dock and was arrested for being an Anabaptist.

Over the next several weeks, he was tortured in an effort to gain information about other Anabaptists he might know. Gerrit continued to confess his faith in Jesus. They tortured him because he had stopped going to the official state church so that he could attend meetings of the Anabaptists. As the torture intensified, they stripped him naked and whipped him with rods until he was nearly unconscious. Then they threw hot then cold water on him. When he came to enough to talk, they blindfolded him, tied his hands behind him, and hung him up by his hands. When none of this broke him, he was put on a rack and stretched out spread eagle. As they tightened the rack, they poured urine in his mouth and put lighted candles under his arms. He refused to betray his brothers and sisters in Christ.

A few days later, he was brought before the city council for sentencing. They sentenced him to death by burning. He was so crippled by the torture that he had to be carried to the stake. Before he was burned, he witnessed to the crowd, "O men, how long is eternity? How long is eternity? But this life here is soon over, yet the conflict here is bitter and strong. But how it still concerns me. O flesh, be patient and stand yet a little, for this is the last struggle." Then he prayed for his accusers and his torturers. "Thou knowest my simple love which is towards Thee. Accept me, and forgive them that inflict this suffering upon me."

CHAPTER 8

PURPOSEFUL IN MY RELATIONSHIP WITH CHRIST

Philippians 3:7–4:1

Twenty years from now you will be more disappointed by the things you didn't do than by the ones you did. So throw off the bowlines. Sail away from the safe shore. Catch the trade winds in your sails. Explore. Dream. Discover.
—Mark Twain

Treasures in heaven are laid up only as treasures on earth are laid down.
—Anonymous

I'VE BEEN BLESSED to meet some great people in my life. Some are famous, a few celebrities, athletes, media personalities, and well-known preachers. Most of the people who have impacted my life are not the famous ones. Oh, it's nice to say I've met them and it's fun to take a picture with them, but to say we are friends would be a stretch. Some of these people have marked me because I admire them. Others have impacted my life because I've read their books. For some, I remember the conversations. A few I "know" because I've met them once or twice, but I would have to remind them of my name even if I do have a face only a mother could love.

While I was serving as executive producer for the Erwin Brothers' film, *Woodlawn*, I got to hang out for a while with several of the main actors. The most famous were Sean Astin (*Lord of the Rings, Rudy*), Sherri Sheppard (*The View*), and Academy Award winner Jon Voight. It was fun to see people on the big screen at ground level.

On another level, I got to know a young man I now consider a friend, Caleb Castille, who played football at Alabama and was the lead character in the movie, Tony Nathan. I've got some great pictures on the sidelines during filming of me with Caleb. Caleb was a member of the Alabama Crimson Tide National Championship team, but he walked away from football to pursue an acting career. Caleb has spoken at Sherwood and is a great young believer.

When Alex Kendrick, Kirk Cameron, and I were on the set of the *Dr. Phil Show* to promote *Fireproof*, we got to spend a few minutes with Dr. Phil. He was very positive, encouraging, and supportive of the film. I've got a great picture of us backstage after the show, but I doubt Dr. Phil has thought about me at all since that day. I've met former President George W. Bush on a couple of occasions, once in the Oval Office and once at an event in Alabama. One of my favorite moments in life is what happened in our exchange in the Oval Office. It's a story for another day, but it is memorable to me. In fact, when I saw him a few years later in Alabama, he immediately asked, "How's the church?" The man has a great mind for names and faces.

While it's fun to talk about these friends and relationships, I'm most grateful for the people that I can say I really know because we've shared life together. Most of their names you wouldn't know. They are the staff members with whom I share ministry at Sherwood, the men in my prayer group, the people in the pews. I'm privileged to know these folks on a deeper level. There is danger in saying we know someone when in fact we really don't. Why? Because we've diluted what it means to be a friend. Name-dropping is one of the favorite American pastimes. "Facebook friends" are often not really our friends. They don't call or even post when we have surgery or a death in the family. It's a trap to judge your life by how many friends or followers you have on social media.

Through the years, because of Sherwood Pictures, I've had a few folks use my name to try to get something from someone. They think because they like Sherwood Pictures that they know me. Because we're one of the largest churches in town, I see people in the community who think they know me. Through the years, I've had requests for money, loans, favors, introductions, book endorsements and movie endorsements from people I've never met. Because they follow me on social media or they've been to a conference I've spoken at, it seems they want me to endorse them on general principles.

My friend Tom Elliff has a great policy on endorsing someone. (By the way, this is a good test of how well you know someone.)

> Over the years, I've noted that there are some guys who are willing to endorse just about any and everything that comes down the pike. After a while their endorsement comes to mean very little. After all, that simple act places a man's reputation in the hands of another. For that reason he'd better know well the person he's recommending . . . not just the content of his book, but the content and character of his life. . . . For the reason above, I am very cautious when endorsing books by men . . . whom I do not know, nor have I been in the ministry trenches with them.[1]

HOW CLOSE ARE YOU FOLLOWING?

I believe the verses before us are Paul's endorsement of the fact that he knew Christ in an intimate way. Because these verses are written in the Holy Bible, which is God-breathed, we could say Jesus endorsed what Paul said about Him. Jesus knew the character of Paul as the apostle was daily controlled by the character of Christ. If we are going to be purposeful people, it begins with a desire to know Christ. In these verses, Paul helps us to understand what it means to know Christ and to have a purposeful relationship with Him. This is not a hot-and-cold, on-and-off relationship with occasional communication. This is not about following Christ from a distance, but saying you're a friend of God. Paul's words here reveal a level of intimacy that is possible for every believer, but few attain it.

The reason believers do not walk in power or with any sense of purpose is that they are often content to follow from a distance. Read these words carefully if you want to understand what purpose in life looks like:

> But whatever things were gain to me, those things I have counted as loss for the sake of Christ. More than that, I count all things to be loss in view of the surpassing value of knowing Christ Jesus my Lord, for whom I have suffered the loss of all things, and count them but rubbish so that I may gain Christ, and may be found in Him, not having a righteousness of my own derived from the Law, but that which is through faith in Christ, the righteousness which comes from God on the basis of faith. (Phil. 3:7–9)

Don't forget what Paul has said in the previous verses. He's given us his religious résumé. In the eyes of the Jews, Paul would have been a candidate for the religious Mount Rushmore. Every entry in his ledger of good words had been an asset, but when he met Christ, his assets became liabilities.

You may recall what the martyred missionary Jim Elliot wrote in 1949: "He is no fool who gives what he cannot keep to gain that which he cannot lose."[2] Paul left behind his heritage, good works, and degrees to pursue Christ. Chuck Swindoll writes about him, "In today's terms, that proud Pharisee known as Saul of Tarsus won all the marbles: the Pulitzer, the Medal of Honor, the Most Valuable Player, the Heisman, the God Medal . . . the Nobel of Ancient Jewry. Had they had newspapers or magazines in this day, his picture would have been on the front page, and the headline would have read, RELIGIOUS ZEALOT OF THE DECADE. He was the name dropped by everybody who was anybody."[3]

Just as he had piled up phrases to show his elite position, Paul now piles up phrases to underscore and emphasize that knowing Christ was all that mattered to him. If you walk back through these verses, you'll see it clearly ("those things I have counted as loss" [3:7]; "I count all things to be loss . . . for whom I have suffered the loss of all things, and count them but rubbish" [3:8]). Obviously Paul's whole worldview had changed. Previously he lived to keep the law, to know the rules, and, before his conversion, to capture and kill Christians. What would he say was his reason for living? "For the sake of Christ" (3:7); "the surpassing value of knowing Christ Jesus my Lord" (3:8); "so that I may gain Christ" (3:8); "found in Him" (3:9); "that I may know Him" (3:10).

J. H. Jowett acknowledges that Paul was willing to "lose the thin and fading robe of reputation if only he can gain the splendid and incorruptible garment of a sanctified character."[4] This fact hinges on three pivot points in this passage: (1) "That I may gain Christ," (2) "That I may know Him," (3) "That I may attain the resurrection from the dead." To say that he wants to gain Christ is a metaphor from the marketplace and business world. Paul wanted to discover his true wealth and riches in Christ Jesus. The riches of gaining Christ meant that all that he had gained in his fleshly efforts was now worth nothing. Paul Rees writes, "Hence we have in Christ the gain of a new perception. 'But whatever gain I had' (in my noble ancestry, my meticulous orthodoxy, my fiercely zealous activity, my silk-smooth, self-won morality), 'I counted as loss . . .' This is Paul's portrayal of profit and loss. There's a new paradigm for the balance sheet of life."[5]

The surpassing value of knowing Christ is a reminder that we aren't followers of a religion; we are in a relationship. In Christ we are in a new position not based on the law, but on love. We are now "in Christ" or "in Him" or "in the Lord." These phrases are used at least 164 times in the New Testament. The Christian life rises and falls on one thing: our union with Christ and our life in fellowship with Christ. The joy of knowing Christ was more important in Paul's mind than anything he had done before knowing Christ. Knowing Christ made the beatings, the persecution, the suffering, the shipwrecks, and the confrontations worth it. His cause was right. His purpose was clear. His passion was Christ.

It's a fascinating study to look at the great heroes of the Bible who knew God. Their writings reveal passion and purpose. In many of their lives, you get glimpses into their battles and their blessings. These men and women knew God. Their spiritual compass was set on true north. They were mostly common people who had an uncommon faith in the living God, which led them to great victories but also cost many of them their lives. Look at church history and you'll see thousands of examples of pastors, missionaries, laymen, revivalists, and evangelists who pursued Christ with passion. They gave their lives to know Christ and make Him known. Study the martyrs, pay attention to those whom we remember and you'll discover none of them had an easy road. It was a hard and narrow road, but it led to victory.

The questions I must ask myself are, "Why am I so easily satisfied with lesser things? Why is, overall, the American church so shallow and carnal? Why are we losing our influence in the culture? Why can't we impact our communities? Why are we losing our youth?" Because we aren't following hard after God. We seem to be content to remain in the kindergarten of faith when God has so much more for us. This is the result of treating our salvation as a privilege and forgetting it also brings responsibility. Paul has already said in 2:12, "So then, my beloved, just as you have always obeyed, not as in my presence only, but now much more in my absence, work out your salvation with fear and trembling." This working out of our salvation speaks of a great responsibility that many of us have abdicated or ignored.

I still remember the first sermon I preached. I surrendered to ministry at a revival in my wife's home church. Once the service was over, I left to find my youth minister, James Miller, who was preaching a revival in another local church. The pastor of that church overheard me telling James I sensed a call to ministry. Right there, on the spot, he asked me to preach in two weeks. I had no clue what I was doing. It was a lousy sermon, but I had a great text. My message that night was from Luke 14 on the cost of discipleship. As I look back over forty years of ministry, discipleship and lordship have been a theme of my ministry and preaching. Paul wasn't interested in knowing *about* Christ; his desire was to know Christ. This is a pursuit of intimacy, friendship, relationship, and communion. We can be Bible students and know a lot about the Bible intellectually but not know the God of the Bible intimately. To know the God of the Bible intimately requires discipleship—recognizing Jesus as Lord and following him as Lord.

In *The Christian's Secret of a Happy Life*, Hannah Whithall Smith writes about this very topic:

> What can be said about man's part in this great work, but that he must continually surrender himself and continually trust? But when we come to God's side of the question, what is there that may not be said as to the manifold and wonderful ways, in which He accomplishes the work entrusted to Him? It is here that the growing comes in. The lump of clay could

never grow into a beautiful vessel if it stayed in the clay pit for thousands of years; but when it is put into the hands of a skillful potter it grows rapidly, under his fashioning, into the vessel he intends it to be. And in the same way the soul, abandoned to the working of the Heavenly Potter, is made into a vessel unto honor, sanctified, and meet for the Master's use.[6]

ETERNITY IN VIEW

To be "found in Him" is a reminder that Paul always had eternity in mind. However, Paul wasn't thinking about a coming day of judgment of his works while on earth. Rather, he was thinking about a coming moment when his faith would be tested and scrutinized. Whether here or there, Paul was focused on living out his faith in a faithful walk. As you dive into these verses, you can get caught up in the positive part of verse 10 and almost ignore the last half. The twenty-first-century American church is allergic to suffering. We avoid it like a plague. Nevertheless, you can't pick and choose which parts of the Bible you want to live in. All of them apply, at some level, to any and all who want to be purposeful in their faith.

". . . that I may know Him and the power of His resurrection and the fellowship of His sufferings, being conformed to His death; in order that I may attain to the resurrection from the dead" (Phil. 3:10–11). Paul is not only talking about the resurrection when Christ returns; he's also talking present tense—God wants us to experience resurrection power now . . . to live in Christ now. This isn't about being able to tell the Easter story. It's so much bigger than knowing a few Bible verses and having a handle on Christian catch words or wearing the latest Christian T-shirt. This is about living out these truths as an active reality in our lives on a daily basis. Paul is talking about experientially, practically living out this truth. The goal is to know Him. This is not some abstract, ambiguous thought. Phillips paraphrases verse 12 well: ". . . grasping ever more firmly that purpose for which Christ grasped me." Weymouth translates it, ". . . striving to lay hold of the prize for which also Christ has laid hold of me."[7] Paul is thinking back to the day when he met Jesus on the road to Damascus. In effect, Jesus struck him down, then picked him up and said, "Saul, you're My man." Since that day, Paul had been living every day of his life as a man on a mission.

When Jesus saved Paul, and us, He had more in mind than getting us a ticket out of hell. He saved us for a purpose. The purpose of our salvation is that we might gain Christ, know Christ, and be found in Christ. This is more than knowing what my spiritual gift is or being able to articulate the blessings I have in Christ. It means, among other things, no longer being concerned with knowing myself or people knowing about me. This is about a passionate pursuit of the One who pursued me. Nothing was more important to Paul. His old life in the flesh was nothing compared to his new life in the Spirit. He counted his religious résumé as loss in verse 7, but in verse 8 he counts everything as loss. Paul calculated what he had given up and he said it was nothing. The greatest of religion was "rubbish" without Christ.

Most Christians know verse 10. In fact, we are familiar with it but not so much intimately acquainted with the depths of its truth. "That I may know Him" or "might be found in Him" implies a power and rightness beyond his ability in the flesh, an appropriated awareness of all things being in Christ. Ernest Campbell notes, "The basis for righteousness under the Law was *doing it*, but the basis of righteousness under grace is *the faithfulness of Christ*."[8]

In chapter 2 Paul wrote of how Christ emptied Himself, laying aside His privileges and prerogatives. He humbled Himself to the lowest place, gave up His rights, and was obedient to death. He chose to die rather than disobey. Knowing Christ is, therefore, about emptying ourselves, humbling ourselves, and obeying God no matter what He asks us to do. It's anywhere, anytime, unconditional obedience. Paul knew Christ:

- He met Him on the road to Damascus (Acts 9).
- Christ was living in Him (Gal. 2:20).
- He lived for Christ (Phil. 1:21).
- Christ was the very essence of his life (Col. 3:3).
- Christ had given him a new life (2 Cor. 5:17).
- He knew Christ as the head of the church (Eph. 1:22–23).

POWER AND SUFFERING IN CHRIST

Paul knew Christ as the source of his power. The word *power* reveals the supernatural dynamic of his life. You see this thought in several of Paul's epistles:

> And He has said to me, "My grace is sufficient for you, for power is perfected in weakness." Most gladly, therefore, I will rather boast about my weaknesses, so that the power of Christ may dwell in me. (2 Cor. 12:9)

> . . . and what is the surpassing greatness of His power toward us who believe. These are in accordance with the working of the strength of His might which He brought about in Christ, when He raised Him from the dead and seated Him at His right hand in the heavenly places. (Eph. 1:19–20)

When he says the words "the power of His resurrection," Paul is revealing spiritual oneness with the risen Christ and all that it implies. It's a power that can be tapped from an endless supply that enables us to carry out God's purpose for our lives. We've been empowered to do what God has called us to do as individual believers and by the Church as a whole. This is supernatural power. Without it, even on our best day, we are spiritually dry. It is the power that comes from the abiding awareness of our need for daily dependence. This is not manpower, political power, or even atomic power; it is greater than all that. The power images of this world cannot compare to the power we have in Christ. Our power flows from the throne of God into the surrendered hearts of His followers. This power enables us to love, forgive, serve, and give ourselves for God's purposes.

Power is a big word in our culture, and many people want it. Power lunch. Power people. Power players. Power teams. But what is the greatest evidence of walking in the power of Christ? How we handle suffering. This is where we lose the average believer. This is why the prosperity gospel and the health-and-wealth preachers are so popular. They tell you the lie that suffering is not part of following Christ. Well if it's not, God owes an apology to the persecuted church throughout the world today! Too many so-called preachers are promising things Jesus never promised His followers. If you read the Gospels, Jesus told them there would be wolves who would attack the sheep and there would be suffering for those who followed. He said, "In this world, you will have tribulation." He told the disciples, "If they persecuted Me, they will persecute you." During the time of Christ, if you saw a man carrying a cross, you knew he wasn't coming back. He was headed to his execution. And Jesus told His disciples, if they wanted to follow Him, they had to "take up their cross."

What about this "fellowship of His sufferings"? Paul writes words that, quite frankly, trouble us. We've bought the lie that to never suffer is the victorious Christian life. Nothing could be further from the truth. Paul wanted us to know that, if we are truly and purposefully pursuing Christ, our stand for Christ will lead to suffering. Phillips paraphrases this as, "I long to share his sufferings." I don't see many hands going up for tough assignments in the kingdom these days. When I was growing up, I would hear the preacher say, "We've been saved to serve." I never heard one say, "We've been saved to suffer." Yet, this is exactly what Paul is saying. You don't see verses like "the fellowship of His sufferings" on many posters or coffee cups!

Jesus may ask you to do what you don't want to do, go where you don't want to go, speak when you don't want to speak, and obey when it would be easier not to. Our flesh rebels at the thought. Christ in us empowers us to embrace that thought.

- Do you bear any scars of battle?
- Does it bother you, the sheer ease of your Christian life?
- Has your identification with Christ cost you anything?
- Do you know the pain of being rejected because you are a Christian?
- Do your friends see you daily taking up your cross?
- Are there any trials, troubles, or times when you felt you were in the middle of turbulence because of your standing with Christ?
- Is your Christian life more than lip service?
- Does your faith lead you to stand against racism and social injustice? To stand for the widow, the orphan, and the poor?
- Does it ever drive you to fast and pray for the persecuted church?

A. W. Tozer wrote, "With the goodness of God to desire our highest welfare, the wisdom of God to plan it, and the power of God to achieve it, what do we lack?"[9] Paul's desire was to be yielded to Christ and so full of the Spirit that Christ might continually and progressively be formed in him. This is, as some people say, "dying daily to self, sin, and Satan. When 'I' is crucified, Christ is crowned." Paul's desire was to one day "reach to the resurrection" because he was sure of his eternal destiny. The words *reach* or *attain* are not words of self-achievement, but a gift given by God. Paul didn't want to appear before God embarrassed, red-faced, or empty-handed. He was zealous for all God had for him, and he wanted to grasp the full purpose for which he had been saved.

"Not that I have already reached the goal or am already fully mature, but I make every effort to take hold of it because I also have been taken hold of by Christ Jesus" (3:12 HCSB). We never arrive. Not in this life. There is more to come. If we are going to be all we have been saved to be in Christ, we need to learn, think, grow, and mature. Too many saints just go to church and leave the same way they came in. They have no intention of growing up, they don't read the Word, and they are saved and stuck. The epistles were written to help the church grow up and become mature in Christ.

It is sad to say, but we are not a nation of thinkers. While we have tons of opinions, we don't think much. Too many believers are Bible school dropouts. They know just enough of the Bible and what God expects of His people to be dangerous.

F. B. Meyer wrote, "Learn to put your hand on all spiritual blessings in Christ and say, 'Mine.'"

Have you settled down in your Christian life? Are you coasting to the finish line? Paul often pictures the Christian life as a race. Paul is in his lane, running his race and pressing toward the finish line. Far too many believers quit before they are done. They retire and lack fire in their bones. The key to running this race, reaching this goal, and attaining maturity is faithfulness and persistence. We don't give up. We don't quit.

There is a race, a goal, an assignment, and a reward. To run a race requires discipline and focus. Paul is not talking about sinless perfection; he is dealing with direction. As my friend Ron Dunn used to say, "We need to pursue holiness so that one day, when we get to heaven, we won't be so shocked."

One of my favorite parts of the old Jay Leno *Tonight Show* was "Jaywalking." Leno would poll random people on the street and ask them questions the average six-year-old should know, and more often than not, the people wouldn't have a clue about the answer. We've all heard preachers say the average church member can't name the twelve disciples or the Ten Commandments. Unfortunately, most can't articulate the message of salvation or the demands on disciples of our Lord to become mature believers.

Do you know God's Word? Do you study it? Do you apply it? Do you know God's will for your life? God's will is found in God's Word, and it is first and foremost to know Christ. After that, your vocation will fall into place. If you're purposefully pursuing the life of Christ and developing the mind of Christ, you'll be on target. Do we truly understand the consequences of not knowing what we should know? Do we fully comprehend the dangers of aimlessly walking through life as if we would get some kind of do-over later on? The consequences of this lack of learning are staggering. We have stunted saints who can't articulate even the ABCs of the faith. Just like teenagers don't think of the consequences of caving in to peer pressure or of a "harmless" post on social media, we seem to be clueless in the realm of spiritual things. Even within the church we are a biblically illiterate society. There are so many examples of this that I don't even have to name them.

As long as some people have been in the church, they still don't know anything about the Word or the consequences of obedience or disobedience. Even though the Bible clearly teaches that we need to be people of prayer, the average believer has an anemic prayer life. We are told to take the gospel to the world, but the overwhelming majority of Christians have never shared their faith. With all the Bible studies, podcasts, conferences, and small groups, you'd think we would be further along than we are.

> Not that I have already reached the goal or am already fully mature, but I make every effort to take hold of it because I also have been taken hold of by Christ Jesus. Brothers, I do not consider myself to have taken hold of it. But one thing I do: forgetting what is behind and reaching forward to what is ahead, I pursue as my

goal the prize promised by God's heavenly call
in Christ Jesus. (Phil. 3:12–14 HCSB)

Mark Batterson's book *All In* opens with the story of missionaries from a century ago who were known as "One Way Missionaries." They purchased one-way tickets to the mission field. Instead of suitcases, they packed a few belongings into coffins. As they set out for sea, they waved good-bye to everyone they loved and everything they knew, knowing they would never return home.

As A. W. Milne, one of those missionaries, set sail for New Hebrides, knowing that headhunters lived there and had martyred every missionary before him, he had no fear. He had already died to himself. For thirty-five years he worked among that tribe. When he died, the tribe buried him in the middle of their village and put this epitaph on his tombstone: "When he came there was no light. When he left there was no darkness." Batterson writes, "When did we start believing that God wants to send us to safe places to do easy things? That faithfulness is holding the fort? That playing it safe is safe? That there is any greater privilege than sacrifice? That radical is anything but normal? . . . It's time to go *all in* and *all out* for the *All in All*."[10]

OUR INCONVENIENT CALLING

It's time for the people of God to admit that we aren't the stuff of which martyrs are made. We've come to accept every-other-week church attendance as faithfulness. We are never stirred by empty altars or dry baptisteries. The average Christian family is more committed to their child's sports league than they are to raising their children in the nurture and admonition of the Lord. What the world of work, athletics, and music would call unacceptable, the church applauds. It is to our shame that we think we've arrived or that half-hearted obedience will be embraced by the living Lord on the day of judgment. Ron Dunn said, "If we are spiritually impoverished, it is not because the hand of grace is tight fisted; it is because the hand of faith is too weak."[11]

Let's not miss God's purpose for our lives. Don't fall prey to perfectionism, and don't quit and be labeled apathetic. If one word could describe us, it should be *passion*. Apathy is rampant in the Christian community. The church starts at eleven o'clock sharp and ends at twelve o'clock dull. The saints are sleeping through the battle. Too many have allowed their perspective to be skewed by watching too much news and not reading enough of the Word. The end result is defeatism. *What's the use? We can't change anything? Let's just give up and pray for the Second Coming.* None of these attitudes line up with "For to me to live is Christ and to die is gain," or "that I may know Him and the power of His resurrection and the fellowship of His sufferings, being conformed to His death."

There is nothing in the New Testament about our calling and commitment being convenient or comfortable. It's a life-long race, a daily wake-up call. When Peter wanted to argue with the Lord about an issue, he ran into an uncompromising Christ. "Then a voice came: 'Go to it, Peter—kill and eat.' Peter said, 'Oh, no, Lord. I've never so much as tasted food that was not kosher.' The voice came a second time: 'If God says it's okay, it's okay'" (Acts 10:13–15 *The Message*). You can't call Jesus Lord and tell Him "no" in the same breath.

We are a nation of quitters. We don't want to pay the price for following Christ. We want to debate, negotiate, take a leave of absence, or even go AWOL. We look for the church with the lowest possible demands on our time and money. It seems we want a full-service God for a welfare Christianity. Jesus said, "Why do you call Me 'Lord, Lord' and do not do what I say?" (Luke 6:46). We've been given a compelling purpose. Paul knew he was a called man. He had a purpose for living and was obligated to that purpose. He was a man with purpose because he was surrendered to Christ. He never thought he did God a favor by responding to the gospel. He was a debtor in passionate pursuit of Christ.

We've inverted the gospel by inviting people to follow us or our favorite doctrine or our denomination. Even worse, we invite Jesus to follow us. We are not the point. Jesus is the point and we are to pursue Him. My friend T. C. Stallings writes in his book, *Playing on God's Team*, "One of the first things a college coach does after signing a new high school recruit to a collegiate team is address any changes that must be made in the player's skills and attributes. It was mutually understood that I could not plan on being a college success while depending on a high school skill set. My new team would require a new me."[12] Are you compelled to compete? Are you clued in as to the cost? Are you competing in the right event? When a coach recruits an athlete, he's taking a chance on an eighteen-year-old kid.

The coach's job, approval ratings, future, and on- and off-the-field success depend on how that athlete responds to the opportunity. With Christ, He has invested everything in us. His name, His church, and His message will be judged by how we live it out. The gospel and Christianity are being measured by the choices, actions, and attitudes of Christians.

I realize we are all a work in progress. But we should be a work with purpose. I've made some lousy investments in my life, things that didn't pan out. I fell for a pyramid scheme one time, and all I got was taken to the cleaners. But I hasten to say, every minute, ministry, dollar, and talent I've invested in living for Jesus has reaped significant dividends. Some of those I won't see until eternity, but I know I've laid up treasures in heaven. While we live in what was once named the fourth poorest city in America, a few years ago our church embarked on a $24 million fundraising campaign. In the process, we've helped plant churches in Baltimore, Cleveland, New Orleans, Long Island City, Burbank, and San Francisco. We've invested in reaching people in multiple nations around the world. We've rebuilt facilities and added new ministry initiatives both at the church and at our Christian school. Why? It's because of the statement that drives us, which hangs on a large banner in our atrium as a constant reminder: Whoever wants the next generation the most will get them.

My wife and I have been blessed to be able to invest because a long time ago, we became obedient in the area of giving. It's part of God's call on our lives, and I believe on the life of every believer, to give sacrificially. If we give of ourselves as the

Macedonians did (2 Corinthians), then giving of our substance is no big deal. The investment we've made will reap dividends for our church for generations to come. In pursuing Christ, we've decided to lay up treasures in heaven. The Christian in America today seems more worried about retirement than eternity. One of the purposes for our lives is to invest in kingdom expansion that will last beyond our lifetime. My mentor, Vance Havner said, "A man is just as rich as his investment in the bank of heaven."

Do you have a compelling purpose? Remember, I'm not asking if you've "arrived" in the Christian life. "Not that I've already reached the goal . . ." You never see a servant of Christ putting themselves on a pedestal. God is not finished with us yet. Our purpose is to know Him. This is personal, not abstract. It's not about comparing ourselves to others and seeing if we are ahead or behind; it's about pursuing Christ while running in our assigned lane. Someone said, "How you live with Christ will determine if you can live for Christ." Alan Redpath observed, "What we do vocationally is nothing but the scaffolding around our lives, which sometimes God has to take away until first He has conquered the core of our being, eliciting our love, worship and conformity to Him."

We need some uncommon Christians today. Nearly ten years ago while I was president of the Southern Baptist Convention Pastors' Conference, I had the privilege of meeting and praying for Tony Dungy. At the time he was head coach of the Indianapolis Colts, and we were meeting for the convention in Indianapolis that year. I got a call from my friend,

Ken Whitten, who knows Tony well. He asked me if I'd like Tony to come to the conference and say a few words. That was one answer I didn't have to pray about! I immediately said yes. About an hour later, I met Tony and Ken behind the stage and was able to introduce Tony to thousands of pastors and leaders that afternoon. He had come straight from practice to say a few words.

Tony Dungy has a purpose in life. It's bigger than his football career, bigger than winning Super Bowl XLI, bigger than being a member of the NFL Hall of Fame. He has found his significance first and foremost in Christ. God made Tony Dungy excel in football, but football is just a platform for him to excel as a believer. I love one story he tells in his book *Uncommon: Finding Your Path to Significance*, about Coach Tom Landry of the Dallas Cowboys:

> The thing that impressed me the most was that although he was a smart, innovative coach who had a great record, he never seemed to be the center of attention. I learned much from him about this core characteristic of humility. He was a quiet man. At times it seemed he was almost shy, but it was simply his humility before God and man. If you probed, he would eventually tell you that he coached the Dallas Cowboys—but that wouldn't be among the first things he talked about.[13]

Later, Dungy continues:

> Coach Tom Landry pointed out that before he began to follow Christ, football was his number one priority; it was his god. His wife and family were somewhere down the list, though he was not sure where. After all, he was earning a living and supporting them—at least financially. However, after he began to walk in a personal relationship with Jesus Christ, he began to redefine his priorities. Next to his relationship with Christ, his family became most important. He continued to excel in coaching football, but it was no longer his number one priority. He wasn't sure which number priority it was, but he made sure that it was always below the priorities of his faith and his family.[14]

If we want to regain our sense of purpose in our relationship with Christ, we must begin, like Coach Landry, to make Christ our number one priority. And like Paul, we must count everything loss for the sake of gaining Christ.

CHAPTER 9

PURPOSEFUL IN STANDING
FOR TRUTH

Philippians 3:7–4:1

The most dangerous of all false doctrine is the
one seasoned with a little truth.
—**Anonymous**

When a half truth is presented as a whole
truth it becomes an untruth.
—**Walter J. Chantry**

THE SOLDIER OF Christ can never take it easy. We are in a battle, and the stakes are eternal. Over the last forty years, I've watched the church slip into a dangerous laziness in our pursuit of God. We aren't discerning and we allow half-truths to seep into our teachings. There are a wide range of "teachers" on radio, television, and podcasts who play around the edges of the truth. They present a half-truth as the gospel truth, and many believers buy it hook, line, and sinker. Ultimately, this leads to factions, groups that break off and become cultish, and divisions in the body that aren't grounded in the Word of God.

A few years ago, someone told me that a certain popular television preacher/best-selling author (I won't name the person) and I were his favorite Bible teachers. I said to him, "That's impossible. The man does not call sin, sin, nor does he even come close to teaching the Word of God as the final authority." Truth, these days, is an endangered species. The preacher or teacher who is purposeful will stand for truth even when it's not popular to do so.

CAN WE KNOW THE TRUTH?

I want to go back and remind you of a few things we covered in a previous chapter. Why? Because we tend to forget the things we need to remember. We have short memories. We sometimes lack discernment. We let our guard down and, before we know it, we are casualties in the spiritual battle.

You cannot read the New Testament without seeing clear teachings regarding heresy, wolves in sheep's clothing, people who seek to undermine the gospel or add to it. Whether

Pharisees, Judaizers, or Gnostics, the early church faced false teachings and teachers that endangered the faith "once for all delivered to the saints." Jesus warned us of false Christs and false prophets in Matthew 24. Paul warned the church of "perilous times" when the love of pleasure, power, fame, and fortune might supplant the love of God. He warned Timothy about seducing spirits, doctrines of demons, and going back to old ceremonial laws. Jesus and the apostles all knew that false prophets would try to deceive the body of Christ.

Whether it comes in the form of blatant heresy, adding to Scripture, or subtle liberalism, the danger is always there. Throughout his entire ministry, Paul was dogged by false teachers seeking to undermine his ministry, corrupt the gospel of grace, and destroy the church. Like any good pastor, Paul was concerned about the health of the church. Many of the wolves he faced are still with us; they just have a new wardrobe. Paul certainly wasn't ignorant of the devices of the devil, who often attacks the church by telling us to exalt tolerance above truth, the head more above the heart; he temps us to stress the positive and ignore the negative by putting happiness above holiness and focusing only on what we want in this world, forgetting the world to come.

Paul used harsh terms for the Judaizers. They were people who sought to impose and enforce a legalistic Christianity that required Gentiles to become Jews before they could become Christians.

Other enemies of the cross were people who lived by no rules. Their concept of Christianity was license—do whatever feels good. Some commentators think these enemies were people in Philippi who marginalized believers for embracing the one true God rather than conforming to the pagan view of many gods. "The legalistic teaching to live according to the law of Moses, had not yet arrived in Philippi, but Paul had learned from experience that it soon would."[1]

Paul was not politically correct. The truth never is. Truth is offensive because it demands we change the way we think. He called these opponents of truth "dogs." He thought of them as half-wild dogs that scavenge for food. Bishop Lightfoot said they were feeding on "the garbage of carnal ordinances."[2] When Paul called these heretics dogs, he turned the tables on them and employed the same word the Jews used to refer to Gentiles. This was an insult of the highest order. To call them "evil workers" was a further insult. In the Old Testament, evil workers were those who did not live by the laws of God. They distorted, debased, and diluted the purity and simplicity of the gospel. Paul further identifies them as the "false circumcision." He branded them as flesh mutilators. Make no mistake about it—to add circumcision, baptism, or any other ritual to salvation is to mutilate the body.

What does this have to do with the church in the twenty-first century? Everything. If anyone tries to earn salvation by works, they deny the New Testament teaching of salvation by grace through faith. Any and all works are insufficient to save us. In truth, works righteousness is driven by the desire of our flesh to feel superior to someone else. It's the mind that thinks, *I'm better than you because I do this or that.* Anyone who teaches works righteousness is arrogant and should be avoided at all costs.

The key is the heart. The basis of faith is grace. Living for Jesus doesn't despise forms; it just refuses to rely on them. We've all been in churches that emphasize the filthy five, the nasty nine, and the dirty dozen. Many of us were raised in legalistic churches where what you wore was more important than who you were inside. Anything added to Christ ultimately takes away from Christ. When Paul writes, "Put no confidence in the flesh" (3:3), it's a clear word of renunciation—don't fall back into thinking you've got anything to offer; don't assume you have anything to add to the simple gospel and the blood of Jesus. Weymouth translates the phrase, "Have no confidence in outward ceremonies."[3] They can't save you or keep you saved. Paul had a past most people would brag about and offer up as the reason they should be on the platform, but he rejected all he had done in the flesh. His heritage, orthodoxy, works, and high morals contributed nothing to his salvation. Prior to his conversion, Paul would have boasted in all that and more . . . but no longer.

Remember what we said earlier—Paul is comparing profits and losses, thinking and calculating in business terms. All his old assets were now liabilities, and he had to write them off because they were worth nothing. John Ruskin says, "I believe that the root of every schism and heresy from which the Christian Church has suffered has been the effort to earn salvation rather than to receive it."

For many walk, of whom I often told you, and now tell you even weeping, that they are enemies of the cross of Christ, whose end is destruction, whose god is their appetite, and whose glory is in their shame, who set their minds on earthly things. For our citizenship is in heaven, from which also we eagerly wait for a Savior, the Lord Jesus Christ; who will transform the body of our humble state into conformity with the body of His glory, by the exertion of the power that He has even to subject all things to Himself. Therefore, my beloved brethren whom I long to see, my joy and crown, in this way stand firm in the Lord, my beloved. (Phil. 3:18–4:1)

ARE YOU STANDING FIRM?

The greatest threat to the church today is a watered-down faith. As Vance Havner used to say, "It's not the woodpeckers but the termites that we need to be worried about." The enemies of the cross of Christ have infiltrated our ranks. The desire among preachers for power, platform, and prestige has resulted in some strange bedfellows in the twenty-first century. We are losing the culture wars because we aren't standing firm in the truth. The church is in retreat because her feet are not shod with the gospel of peace. Some have even laid down their weapon, the sword of the Spirit, and surrendered. Paul commands the church to stand firm. It's a military term that carries the idea of holding your ground in the face of an onslaught.

1. Stand firm in the FAITH (1 Cor. 16:13).
2. Stand firm in FREEDOM (Gal. 5:1—don't go back to the bondage of the law).
3. Stand firm in the FELLOWSHIP (Phil. 1:27—live in harmony and unity).
4. Stand firm in the FAMILY (Phil. 4:1—stand together with your brothers and sisters in Christ).
5. Stand firm in the FOUNDATIONS (2 Thess. 2:15—stay with the Word).
6. Stand firm in the FIGHT (Eph. 6:11).

Vance Havner wisely observed, "The church is not developing her recruits into disciplined soldiers. We are fighting the greatest battle of all time with the most untrained army on earth. If strict discipline is necessary in art and athletics, how can we expect to be advanced Christians and stay in kindergarten?"[4] Let's be honest—are we discerning of the wolves that seek to sneak into our churches? Are we resisting the enemy? Are we even aware we're in a wrestling match? Are we fighting the good fight of faith? Do we recognize the forces trying to knock us off balance or make us casualties of war?

As a pastor, it breaks my heart when people leave the church. Some leave because they don't want to live up to the demands of Scripture. They find a place where serving is easier and the truth is watered down. Some leave because they get mad over something. Unfortunately, some have left and followed teachings that are contrary to the clear revelation of Scripture. In my first five years in Albany, we lost hundreds of people to other churches. Some left because I didn't preach from the King James Version. Others left because I confronted the obvious legalism in the church (no clapping, women couldn't wear pants, and a dozen other things). They thought they were a Bible-believing church. Unfortunately, it didn't take me long to figure out they believed the Bible, plus a few rules the Pharisees would have been proud of. I preached for almost a year out of the book of Galatians to walk the church through the foolishness of legalism.

I'm not a great Bible teacher, but I know what my responsibility is as a pastor. When Paul writes, "according to the pattern" (3:17), he is using a term that means to strike an exact image upon a blank piece of metal. It was a term for making coins or cutting out a pattern to make a garment. He warns the church over and over: "I often told you." This wasn't the first time they had heard these warnings. They were to continually guard their hearts and minds in Christ. Paul nailed it when he described these false teachers who live for sensual pleasure. This can be sensuality in the way we normally think of it. It can also be one whose focus is on lusting after experiences and feelings. They want the thrill of the fill. They want feelings instead of the filling of the Spirit. They judge worship subjectively. They exalt gifts over the Giver. When this happens, truth has been abandoned and they are feeding at the trough of junk food.

Because their god is their appetite, they are constantly trying to feed off anything or everything other than Christ. I was at breakfast recently with several local pastors. One of them told me, "I've got people in my church who get more excited if we get a member from your church than if we have lost people visiting." As a pastor, I've seen it all. We've had churches court our members to change their membership by promising them they could have a leadership position or serve on a key committee. I've watched pastors visit our members in nursing homes, promising them they'll take better care of them than our church. These kinds of vultures and wolves aren't interested in reaching a community; they are only concerned with stealing sheep.

There are many like this—it's not just a few here and there. Paul is not saying, "If you live long enough, you'll probably bump into a few of them." He's saying, "Open your eyes; they are all around you." Why are these people a danger? Because they produce a watered-down faith or some form of acceptable idolatry. They make something or someone other than Jesus the focus of faith and life. A counterfeit always looks real until you put it up against the real thing. If you want to be able to detect counterfeit bills, you learn what a legitimate bill looks like—you become so familiar with the real that you can quickly detect the false.

Another danger is found in those who abuse the grace of God. They live as they want, rejecting authority and ignoring the fact that grace doesn't mean you are free to do what you please. Grace means you are free not to sin. "What shall we say then? Are we to continue in sin so that grace may increase? May it never be! How shall we who died to sin still live in it? . . . Even so consider yourselves to be dead to sin, but alive to

God in Christ Jesus" (Rom. 6:1–2, 11). They minimize sin and the standards of God, and their leaders are easy to identify: "For such men are slaves, not of our Lord Jesus Christ but of their own appetites; and by their smooth and flattering speech they deceive the hearts of the unsuspecting" (Rom. 16:18). Some folks go to bars to get their kicks, and some go to church. When the mosh pit becomes a priority over the altar, you've got a problem. When entertainment is the goal of the church, you've lost the biblical high ground. I'm not talking about styles of worship here; I'm talking about whom the worship is focused on. Worship and the Word must be inseparable. I love R&B and soul music. I love the Motown sound of the sixties. But soulish and spiritual are not the same thing—soulish stirs the emotions, but spiritual, regardless of the style, changes the heart and mind.

Let me make some basic applications of what becomes acceptable when our appetite is our god. We will no longer be servants; rather, we will serve if it's convenient, and makes us look good. We will look for ways to bail out, back off, and make excuses. We will totally ignore the clear teachings of the Word regarding evangelism and stewardship, and the Great Commission will be optional. We will make church more about having my cup of coffee than offering a cup of cold water in the name of Jesus. In our flesh, we love preachers and teachers who let us get away with this kind of nonsense. One of the greatest dangers to your faith is to evaluate the success of a service by how you felt about it. God can work in silence or in shouting. Jesus was never impressed with enthusiasm—the same crowd that shouted "Hosanna!" one day was shouting "Crucify Him!" a few days later. Vance Havner said, "We reward, coax, picnic, persuade, tantalize—trying to get church members to come to church. We have tried banners, seals, diplomas, badges, buttons and pot luck dinners to try to induce people to do what they ought to do because they love God."[5]

Paul also says "they are enemies of the cross" (Phil. 3:18). They don't want to talk about sacrifice or dying to self. When a believer is compromised, he's an enemy of God. James named three enemies of God: the world, the flesh, and the devil. The world has a gradual, gravitational pull on us. Friendship with the world leads to compromise, and compromise ultimately results in loving this world and conforming to it. The flesh, our old way of living, is bent toward sin. When we live in the flesh, we are grieving the Holy Spirit. The devil is the most obvious enemy of the cross. He wants us to love the world and live according to our flesh. If he can't keep you from being saved, he will try to destroy your testimony. He works to undermine. He sets traps for us. He baits us so that he can lure us in. He has his minions who often counsel us to "lighten up," "don't take your faith so seriously," "God loves you, so live like you want."

"Certain persons have crept in unnoticed, those who were long beforehand marked out for this condemnation, ungodly persons who turn the grace of our God into licentiousness and deny our only Master and Lord, Jesus Christ" (Jude 4). Jude was aware of those who had crept in like false prophets, who said God would never judge His people because He loves them. The *IVP Background Commentary* notes, "Biblical grace means forgiveness and the power to overcome sin, not permission to act immorally." We are held responsible for the purity and integrity of the faith delivered to us. Our cause is great, and it has eternal significance for us and for this lost world. The world needs to see in us a pure faith, confident that we have been called to be salt and light. They also need the people of God to be serious about propagating the gospel. The Great Commission to reach, teach, and disciple is not optional, nor is it limited to preachers and missionaries. It's an "all call."

These false teachers are headed toward a disastrous end—"whose end is destruction" (Phil. 3:19). Phillips translates, "These men are heading for utter destruction," and The Message paraphrases, "easy street is a dead-end street." Even worse, they boast in this behavior. Glorying in shame used to be limited to brothels and bars, but now it's in the church. We excuse, ignore, and embrace sin that should be dealt with. The world in which we live looks for churches that will exalt what God condemns. We are criticized for confronting sexual sin, but, given the teachings of the Word of God, we have no option. Those who embrace godless perversion are not open-minded; they are demonically deceived. We are seeing clear evidence today of churches embracing lifestyles that Paul condemned in the book of Romans. We are ordaining people and applauding them because of their deviant lifestyles and allowing them to stand in pulpits and preach the Bible according to their perverted interpretation.

There are many images of the church in the New Testament. We are a family, a building, a body, a bride, an army. As citizens of heaven, we are to fight for the advancement of the gospel. We are in the world, but not of the world, and we should be distinctively different. Roman citizens could be spotted in any city because they had a certain dress, manner of speech, and diet. Even if they moved to a new town, they continued to follow Roman law and practice. When we blend in, it means we aren't standing out. Some churches want to sing, look, and act like the world. Why would people of the world give up their only day off to come to a church that isn't distinctively different from the world they live in six days a week? Church shouldn't be boring, but it should never be compromised to get a crowd.

Notice the contrast between those whose god is their belly and the people of God who are waiting for the Lord Jesus: ". . . who will transform the body of our humble state into conformity with the body of His glory, by the exertion of the power that He has even to subject all things to Himself" (Phil. 3:21). Alec Motyer writes, "The forces of nature, the ordered universe, the unbelieving hearts of men, spiritual wickedness in heavenly places, the prince of the power of the air; mention any opponent to the return of Christ and Scripture will nullify its opposition by the power that subdues all things. . . . It is this power which underwrites the promise of His coming again."[6] We have a purpose for being here. We aren't aimlessly wandering around waiting for the Second Coming. We are on mission, and we have our assignment.

Having traveled numerous times to Israel, I'm always impressed with their soldiers. Both men and women are required to enlist at age eighteen, and then they serve in the reserves for a number of years. They know where to report if there's an emergency, and they know what to do and what to look for. They are trained to live with impending danger because of where they live.

Often, you'll see Israeli soldiers in uniform at tourist sites. Part of their training is to learn their nation's history. They are taught what they are fighting for and why they are to prepare for the battle. The nation's leaders want them to understand that there is no victory without preparation, knowledge, and appreciation for the freedom they've been given.

"Therefore . . . stand firm." In Colossians, Paul reminds the church to walk "in Him," meaning we take Jesus as our boundary. Everything we need to walk in spirit and truth is in Christ. We don't have to go outside of Christ to find what we need. I was born in Mississippi; my wife, Terri, and my oldest daughter, Erin, were born in Georgia; and our youngest daughter, Hayley, was born in Texas. I tell folks I'm Mississippi mud with two Georgia peaches and a Texas rose! No matter where we go or what we do, we cannot deny our roots. We are who we are because of where we were born, who we were born to, and our DNA. What changes us is when we are born again in Christ. Then the old passes away and the new comes. We are to be ever learning what it means to live for Christ.

I don't have to add anything to Jesus to live in victory and walk in power. I don't need to buy some bottle of snake oil or trinket to find power. I don't have to read the latest book by some best-selling author. I have what I need in Christ. I have who I need in Christ. I have all I need in Christ. Every word in your Bible is written with one of twenty-six letters of the alphabet—you don't have to get beyond your ABCs to know what God has for you! In Christ alone are the supernatural resources necessary to stand firm.

Paul begins chapter 4 with a word we've seen several times in Philippians: *therefore.* Once again, we'll ask, "What is it there for?" Paul is building on what he has previously written:

- In light of these enemies of the cross . . .
- In light of our heavenly citizenship . . .
- In light of the soon coming of Jesus . . .

He expects us to act accordingly. Lehman Strauss wrote, "The previous chapter concluded with the reminder of the all-sufficiency of the power of God to meet any and every emergency in this life as well as to effect the complete and final change of our bodies in preparation for the life which is to come."[7] Paul is speaking as a man "in Christ" who has personally practiced the discipline of "standing firm." Believers are going to be pushed around, so the question is, "What do we do when that happens?"

POWER FOR CHURCH UNITY

For some reason, the Philippians struggled to deal with issues in the church. Paul reminds them that the same power is available to them whether they are dealing with false teaching, false witnesses, gossips, or troublemakers. All of these are issues, in Paul's mind, that threatened the unity, health, and growth of the church. "Therefore" becomes the link between God's power and man's problem. Don't let a heretic bully you.

Over and over in Philippians, Paul uses the word *brethren* because he's talking to his church family (1:12; 3:1, 13, 17; 4:8). Paul loved these people and longed to see them again. If one day he were able to return, he wanted to find a vibrant fellowship. A few weeks ago I was talking to someone from my hometown. The church I grew up in used to have six hundred to eight hundred people on Sunday. Today, they are down to less than a dozen . . . and the sanctuary seats a thousand. I can't bear to go back there. Most of the folks I knew have already passed away, but I wish I could ask, "What happened?" Back in the nineties I did a revival in my home church. The last message I preached there was titled, "If I Were Your Pastor." The pastor I grew up under was present that night. I reminded them of their past and tried to speak the truth in love, but honestly I was angry and broken-hearted about what had happened to a church where I had repeatedly seen the power of God move and work. That night, the only children in the nursery were mine. They had no children, no youth. It was just a bunch of gray-haired people singing "Victory in Jesus" when it was obvious they were a defeated bunch. I've often wondered what happened. Why did they quit caring about the next generation?

Paul loved this church and had invested heavily in it. Like any biblical leader, he sometimes had to rebuke, correct, and exhort. A pastor is a shepherd, but a shepherd doesn't hold the hands of his sheep; he uses his rod and staff to keep them in line. Problems are a part of life. I often joke with my preacher friends, "Pastoring would be great if it weren't for people!" The truth is, I'm one of the people, and if I'm not careful, I too will get in the way of the truth. Paul begins chapter 4 by reminding the Philippians (and us) that when we ignore problems or problem people, we are setting the church up for failure. Problems don't go away if you ignore them. They won't disappear if you close your eyes and pretend they don't exist. Compromise and conflict must be confronted. Left alone, nothing stays the same.

I remember hearing Jim Cymbala say that when folks join his church, he will welcome them, love them, and disciple them regardless of their situation in life. No matter what they've been through or what they're going through, he will show them the love of Christ—it doesn't matter. But, he said, if you cause disunity in the church, he will not let you get away with it. The devil often sends troublemakers into a church to see if we have the guts to deal with them. Sometimes people are just carnal and want their way and whine when they don't get it. Either way, we don't have an option. We are to stand against the enemy and his tactics, no matter what form they take. I refuse to surrender to cynics or to allow gossips to rule the day.

I think some folks have the spiritual gift of pouting, whining, fussing, and fighting. When I see kids acting like that, I expect the parents to step up and discipline. When I see church members acting like that, it is part of the calling of deacons and certainly the calling of the pastor to say, "That's not going to happen here." Know this: church discipline and correction are not options in a church buffet line. If problems are not confronted with truth, there will be no stability in the church. The position from which Paul confronts the two women in Philippi is, "in the Lord"—in God's power. In other words, Paul is not trying to make things easier for himself, but he is concerned about the reputation of the church before a watching world.

Paul names the women, and their names indicate they weren't living up to their identity (Phil. 4:2). *Euodia* means "fragrant and prosperous journey," and *Syntyche* means "fortunate." These two ladies were stinking up the church! Paul calls them to live up to their names. The church already knew the problem with these two women. Now Paul writes, under the inspiration of the Holy Spirit, to give us the names of two women who had long and loose tongues. Paul says, "Live in harmony in the Lord." He's encouraging these believers to be of the same mind, to think the same way. We don't know the specifics; the issue could have been personal or doctrinal. Regardless, Paul confronts them to get on the same page. Get over yourselves. Church is not about you.

People often say, "We will agree to disagree," but that's not always biblical. In 2 Corinthians 13:11, Paul orders the church to "think the same thing" (NIV). There is a way to deal with disagreements that pleases God. There is no purpose without a standard of what that purpose should look like. Forget preferences—the standard is truth as revealed in the Word. Jesus doesn't disagree with Himself. He's not at odds with Himself. The Father, Son, and Spirit are one. Paul told the Colossians to "let the peace of Christ rule in your hearts . . . you were called in one body" (3:15). Paul doesn't pick sides. He says, "Both of you need to die to yourself and get right with God and one another."

For Paul, unity was a big, big deal.

> Only conduct yourselves in a manner worthy
> of the gospel of Christ, so that whether I come
> and see you or remain absent, I will hear of you
> that you are standing firm in one spirit, with
> one mind striving together for the faith of the
> gospel. (Phil. 1:27)

> . . . make my joy complete by being of the same
> mind, maintaining the same love, united in
> spirit, intent on one purpose. (Phil. 2:2)

> . . . let us keep living by that same standard to
> which we have attained. (Phil. 3:16)

He previously referred to his own response to those who opposed him. He confronts this disagreement quickly—get it right, come to terms, and move on. "Indeed, true companion, I ask you also to help these women who have shared my struggle in the cause of the gospel, together with Clement also and the rest of my fellow workers, whose names are in the book of life" (4:3). He appeals for a mature mediator (whose name we do not know) to step in and get this issue solved. The term *true companion* literally means "yokefellow." The term is an adjective, not a noun, indicating the character of the person he is referring to. A yokefellow was a crossbar with loops on the end through which the heads of two oxen would be placed. Paul says, "We are yoked together, brother. Help me out here." The request was simple: "Help them." It's a verb used of seizing, conceiving, or taking hold of something. This could have been the pastor, overseer, elder, or key leader in the fellowship—quite possibly the person who actually read the letter to the church when it came from Paul. In every conflict, someone has to step up and take the bull by the horns. To the Galatians, Paul wrote, "You who are spiritual, restore . . ." (6:1). To stand in the truth, you have to stand for the truth. Spiritually minded people will put truth over feelings. These women had once been useful for the kingdom, but they had gotten off track. They had made a difference; now they are causing a train wreck. Paul wants them restored to their former usefulness.

Sadly, Christians and churches lose focus when they think the focus should be on them or their preferences. Our greatest hindrance in the church today is in our own ranks. We provide the enemy with ammunition to cut us down. Vance Havner wrote, "It is sometimes argued that hospitals minister to sick people and schools to ignorant people and the church to sinful people; therefore we should not set too high a standard for our church members. But sick people are expected to get well, and ignorant people are supposed to learn, and Christians should grow and become better. There is no excuse for us to stay babes on milk when we should mature and feed on meat."[8]

The Life Application Bible Commentary notes,

> In any group of people—from churches to bowl-
> ing leagues—offenses will occur and pride will
> get hurt. The difference between churches and
> other groups is that pride should not control a

situation. Christians should be eager to forgive, forget, and go on. Many Christians lack the humility or the motivation to deal with hurts and slights in the proper way. Grudges go on for years, gossip makes mountains of anthills, and hard feelings become like pillars—just part of the architecture. No one in the church should be expected to agree with everyone else on every issue facing the group, except one, the most important: Jesus is Lord. Around that wonderful common keynote, the harmonies of a thousand different voices sing. If you hold a grudge against someone in the church, settle it today. Find common ground in Jesus. Make reconciliation and get your Christian service back to full strength.[9]

Be of humble mind, laying aside all haughtiness, and pride, and foolishness, and angry feelings . . . being especially mindful of the words of the Lord Jesus which He spake, teaching us meekness and long-suffering.
—Clement of Rome

CHAPTER 10

PURPOSEFUL IN PRAISE AND PRAYER

Philippians 4

That which God abundantly makes the subject of his promises, God's people should abundantly make the subject of their prayers.
—**Jonathan Edwards**

IN ORDER TO live with purpose, we must know how those who came before us thought and prayed. The pages of Scripture are marked with examples of God's people in prayer. Their prayers influenced the way they thought, acted, and reacted.

IS PRAYER IN YOUR DNA?

Paul bookends this short letter with prayer. Obviously prayer was an integral part of the DNA of the local church. We talk about prayer in the church, but we do little of it. Prayer is often nothing more than a bridge between songs or something we do while the ushers come forward to take the offering.

My friend Gary Miller leads a ministry called, "Talk Less, Pray More." In commenting on Acts 6, he writes, "Those who wish to reconnect the contemporary church to its ancient root system need to take a close look at what the early church fathers did. The early church was divided, and the gap between the two groups was widening with consistent complaints of mistreatment. The solution selected by the twelve should be a prototype for every church experiencing conflict. The twelve appointed themselves to prayer and the ministry of the Word."[1] I can name a hundred churches I know in conflict, but I'd be hard pressed to name ten with a vital and viable intercessory prayer ministry.

Your praying affects your thinking, and your thinking affects your praying. When any believer gets their prayer life in order, they will begin to think with the mind of Christ. Prayer is more than asking God to run errands for us. Prayer trusts in God to do what He says. When our prayers are in harmony with the Father, we begin to embrace prayer as the breath of faith. The praying church is a formidable force standing against the world, the flesh, and the devil.

Paul was not praying over a cup of coffee at the local bistro. He was in prison facing martyrdom. The culture was overrun by paganism, and the church was under attack by people with agendas inconsistent with the Word of God. Opposition and persecution were on the rise, coupled with strained relationships inside the church, as we saw in the previous chapter. Paul wants to make sure the church gets on track and stays on track.

Karen Mains wrote a parable titled "A Brawling Bride." She describes a wedding ceremony where the groom is dressed in a spotless tuxedo. He is handsome and smiling, anxiously awaiting his bride. Everyone is in place, the family is seated, and the moment arrives. The organist begins the wedding march. Everyone rises to look toward the bride, and a gasp fills the room. The bride limps down the aisle, her dress tattered and torn. There are cuts and bruises all over her. Her nose is bleeding, she has a black eye, and her hair is a mess. Mains writes, "Does this handsome groom deserve better than this?" And then the clincher, "Alas, His bride, The Church, has been fighting again."[2]

In his classic book *Well-Intentioned Dragons*, Marshall Shelley writes, "Within the church, there are often sincere, well-meaning saints but they leave ulcers, strained relationships, and hard feelings in their wake . . . they are loyal church members, convinced they are serving God, but they wind up doing more harm than good. They can drive pastors crazy . . .

or out of the church."[3] Sound like anyone you know? Does that look like the person you see in the mirror every morning?

The bride of Christ has abandoned the altar of obedience and surrender. We pray, not for the glory of God, but for God to meet our demands. We are anxious, fearful, prayerless, and powerless. We've lost the high ground of the praying ground.

If we are going to reach the world with the gospel, the church has to get her act together. Before the church was sent out to fulfill the Great Commission, she was sent to an upper room to pray until power fell from on high. Prayer and then power led to the church penetrating the city. If the devil can't get Christians fighting among themselves, he will work to get them to ignore prayer. Both will render the church ineffective.

I find it strange, yet not so strange, that Paul immediately follows a few verses about two women fighting with verses on praise and proper thinking. If you've never lived through a church fight, consider yourself blessed. Some folks have lived with church fights so long that they think the purpose of gathering is to fight.

The Bible is clear on what God thinks about how we use our tongues. The tongue is attached to the brain. What we say comes from the well inside of us. Is your tongue an instrument of praise or cursing? Do your words and deeds bless others or cause them to cringe when they are around you?

James warns us about the tongue:

> And the tongue is a fire, the very world of iniq-
> uity; the tongue is set among our members as

that which defiles the entire body, and sets on
fire the course of our life, and is set on fire by
hell. For every species of beasts and birds, of
reptiles and creatures of the sea, is tamed and
has been tamed by the human race. But no one
can tame the tongue; it is a restless evil and full
of deadly poison. With it we bless our Lord and
Father, and with it we curse men who are made
in the likeness of God; from the same mouth
come both blessing and cursing. My brethren,
these things ought not to be this way. Does a
fountain send out from the same opening both
fresh and bitter water? Can a fig tree, my brethren, produce olives or a vine produce figs? Nor
can salt water produce fresh.

Who among you is wise and understanding?
Let him show by his good behavior his deeds in
the gentleness of wisdom. But if you have bitter jealousy and selfish ambition in your heart,
do not be arrogant and so lie against the truth.
This wisdom is not that which comes down
from above, but is earthly, natural, demonic.
For where jealousy and selfish ambition exist,
there is disorder and every evil thing. But the
wisdom from above is first pure, then peace-
able, gentle, reasonable, full of mercy and good
fruits, unwavering, without hypocrisy. And

the seed whose fruit is righteousness is sown in
peace by those who make peace. (3:6–18)

The *IVP New Testament Commentary* notes, "If Paul had written this passage, we might expect him to employ his image of the church as the body of Christ to describe the injury done to other lives by one person's impure speech. But James's reference to the body appears to be in the Jewish sense of the whole person rather than a figure of speech for the church. His focus is more on the destruction of the impure speaker's own life. We can envision how this might be so. Spread gossip, and people will not trust you. Speak with sarcasm and insults, and people will not follow you. Yet what is especially on James's mind is not the reaction of others to your speech but the spreading of sin from your speech to the rest of your life. Be hateful with your tongue, and you will be hateful with other aspects of your behavior. If you do not discipline and purify your speech, you will not discipline or purify the rest of your life."[4]

I've personally experienced the damaging effects of an uncontrolled tongue. It leads to anger, bitterness, gossip, and division, and sometimes it even destroys a person's health. It is definitely a cancer that can destroy the body of Christ in a local setting. In my first full-time church position, I was filling the pulpit for the pastor and a deacon came up after the service and tried to punch me. Another called one night and wanted to meet in my front yard and fight me. The blame for the powerless church in America lies not outside the church, but within her. It's not because we do not have freedom to worship, assemble, preach, and pray. It's because stinkin' thinkin' is more prevalent than the mind of Christ.

Let's purposefully choose that we will not be the kind of people who are known for fighting, arguing, and dividing a church. We can't afford to let negative people influence us. I heard a story about a young pastor who had two ladies in the church who were always griping and complaining. He called an older pastor and asked, "How can I be positive? How can I keep a good attitude with those two in the church?" The older pastor said, "Get down on your knees and thank God you aren't married to one of them!"

REJOICE IN THE LORD!

One of my best friends is Dr. Charles Lowery. Charles is a psychologist who travels the country speaking to businesses and ministries. I've often said that he's my personal psychiatrist. He keeps me sane and grounded. In one of his messages, he told a story that helped my perspective about how to respond to crises in life. A lady was married to a colonel in the Army who was stationed in Germany, and she was going to meet him with their nine kids in tow. She got to customs with the suitcases, carry-on luggage, and tickets. The customs agent asked her, "Ma'am, do all these children belong to you?" She said, "Yes, they are all mine." Then he asked, "Do you have any weapons, contraband, or drugs in your possession?" She said, "Sir, if I had any of those things, don't you think I would have used them by now?"

We've tried everything to get through life except following the instructions. We know these verses, but do we pray them over our lives?

> Rejoice in the Lord always; again I will say, rejoice! Let your gentle spirit be known to all men. The Lord is near. Be anxious for nothing, but in everything by prayer and supplication with thanksgiving let your requests be made known to God. And the peace of God, which surpasses all comprehension, will guard your hearts and your minds in Christ Jesus. (Phil. 4:4–7)

Negative thinking allows my old nature—my flesh—to control me. Speaking negatively violates these truths. In these verses we see how we should think when we get out of bed, how we should treat the people we meet during the day, and how we should address problems. Ron Dunn noted that these verses can be divided into an easy-to-remember outline:

- A praise list (v. 4)
- A prayer list (v. 6)
- A ponder list (v. 8)
- A practice list (v. 9)

Paul had experienced great difficulties, but he never lost his ability to rejoice in the Lord. Remember, you're not alone on this journey. We can rejoice in the Lord because we know who He is and whose we are. The devil thought God was not worthy of praise. God scoffs in the face of the enemy when He takes a fallen man and turns him into a God worshiper. It's true of the psalmist. Even in hard times, he ultimately comes back to praising God. The psalmist praised God by faith regardless of his circumstances. We rejoice by faith because the Lord is near. His Spirit is within us, and He is coming back for us. When sinners saved by grace rejoice in the Lord, no matter what comes their way, it's a reminder to the devil that he made the wrong choice.

Our rejoicing is in the Lord. We will always have circumstances that cause us to question, doubt, and even fear. But when we rejoice "in the Lord," we look up to Him instead of looking around at our situation. Look back at Philippians 1:19: "I know that this will turn out for my deliverance through your prayers and the provision of the Spirit of Jesus Christ." Paul believed when all was said and done, God was going to work it all out. No matter what happened, he chose to rejoice.

We are either rejoicing or we aren't. The reason our corporate worship seems so hollow is that we don't worship privately. Sometimes we borrow trouble. We stress about things we can't control. To learn to rejoice is to learn to get on top of all that is dragging you down and stand on the promises of God. There are seasons in life when rejoicing doesn't come easily. Yet we are still commanded to rejoice. With the command comes the power to obey. Rejoicing should be demonstrative, stimulating your own mind and the minds of others to follow suit. Joy is contagious. This is not rejoicing in our circumstances or even in answered prayer, healing, or deliverance. It is rejoicing "in the Lord."

And we should rejoice "always." No matter what's going on in your life, you can rejoice. Why? Because it's not about you—it's about Him. And He is in control of how the story ends. In fact, He's already promised us good news in His Word!

Paul was a man of rejoicing. He had every reason, with all he had been through, to whine and complain. Yet joy was his duty and delight. Someone wrote, "The calendar of the sinner has only a few days in the year marked as festival days; but every day of the Christian's calendar is marked by the hand of God as a day of rejoicing."[5]

We all know people who don't rejoice. They see a dark cloud rather than the silver lining. They would find something to complain about no matter what good came their way. When I was growing up, we had a lady who worked in my dad's drugstore for a few years. My dad taught me to be polite, so when she came to work on Saturdays I would ask how she was doing. The rest of the day was spent listening to a laundry list of all the problems she was having. Finally one day, my dad said, "Don't ever ask her how she's doing again!"

"Rejoice in the Lord always." Let's admit that it's easier said than done. But it's a command. This doesn't mean we hide our heads in the sand. It is an act of faith from an eternal outlook. We don't evaluate Scripture in light of our circumstances. We evaluate our circumstances in light of Scripture. We should rejoice always because God will ultimately triumph over every situation of life. Whatever God brings into our lives, He alone is adequate for the day. He is working out His purpose.

Do not fret because of evildoers,

Be not envious toward wrongdoers.

For they will wither quickly like the grass

And fade like the green herb.

Trust in the Lord and do good;

Dwell in the land and cultivate faithfulness.

Delight yourself in the Lord;

And He will give you the desires of your heart.

Commit your way to the Lord,

Trust also in Him, and He will do it.

He will bring forth your righteousness as the light

And your judgment as the noonday.

Rest in the Lord and wait patiently for Him;

Do not fret because of him who prospers in his way,

Because of the man who carries out wicked schemes.

Cease from anger and forsake wrath;

Do not fret; it leads only to evildoing.

For evildoers will be cut off,

But those who wait for the Lord, they will inherit the
land.

Yet a little while and the wicked man will be no more;

And you will look carefully for his place and he will
not be there.

But the humble will inherit the land

And will delight themselves in abundant prosperity.

(Ps. 37:1–11)

The psalmist reminds us we aren't supposed to fret. That word means "to burn up or get heated up." We are to praise God when our natural bent is to panic. If we want to learn to rejoice, the steps to living this kind of life are given to us in this psalm.

- Trust in the Lord (v. 3).
- Delight in the Lord (v. 4).
- Commit yourself to the Lord (vv. 5–6).
- Rest in the Lord (v. 7).

These truths teach us to develop a godly perspective. The temporary evil will one day be gone. Those who oppose the work of Christ may not know it, but their end is coming.

If I don't learn to trust God, I won't find it possible to praise Him. My security is not in my circumstances but in the sovereign Lord. Those who are living in lands where Christians are persecuted seem to be more free in their praise and worship than those of us who have the freedom to do so without fear of the consequences. Why? They have an eternal perspective. To rejoice is to delight. The word *delight* comes from a root that means "to be brought up in luxury, to be pampered." David is praising God for the abundance of blessings we have in the Lord. Here is one of the great dangers of the prosperity gospel—it leads us to enjoy the blessings and minimize the One who blesses, the Lord. Warren Wiersbe says, "If we truly delight in the Lord, then the chief desire of our heart will be to know Him better so we can delight in Him even more, and the Lord will satisfy that desire!"[6]

The person who is purposeful in rejoicing has also learned to "rest in Him." They've committed their ways to the Lord, meaning they've rolled off their burdens onto the Lord. Jesus said, "Come to Me, . . . and I will give you rest" (Matt. 11:28). This is not the kind of rest we get when we take a sleeping pill, but the kind of rest that God brings to our inner being. Resting in the Lord refers to being silent and still before Him. Sometimes I find myself too busy for God and I forget Him during the day. I rejoice that when I forget Him, He does not forget me. This is a hard one for me because I like noise. I get restless if I'm not doing something. I'm guilty of often grabbing my phone to talk, text, or check social media because I can't "be still and know that He is God." When I know He is God and I'm not, I can rest . . . and rejoice. David shows us the wisdom of maturity. After a lifetime of reflecting on all he had been through, he says, "Trust . . . delight . . . commit . . . rest."

There was a little girl who had a praying mom. Her mom was one of those folks you see who are just full of Jesus. Their countenance shows a contentment and peace most long for. One day the little girl snuggled up to her mom who was sitting on the couch with her eyes closed in prayer. She wasn't praying out loud, but the little girl knew she was praying. After a long time of silence, she whispered in her mom's ear, "Mother, is this doing anybody any good?" We've all been there, wondering if our praying is doing any good.

Tell Jesus. He will see you through. That's what Paul is telling us to do. That's what David was telling us to do. Think about it: the best atmosphere for prayer is praise. Too often we are hot in prayer and cold in praise. We do five times more asking than we do praising and adoring the Lord for who He is. Andrew Bonar recognized, "I have never sufficiently praised the Lord, and never can. . . . We should always wear the garment of praise, not just waving a palm-branch now and then."[7] Sometimes, in prayer, we are really saying in our hearts, "Listen Lord, your servant is speaking!" rather than, "Speak Lord, your servant is listening." When I listen, I learn to rejoice.

ANXIOUS ABOUT NOTHING

When Paul writes, "Be anxious for nothing, but in everything by prayer and supplication with thanksgiving let your requests be made known to God" (4:6), he is stretching his readers (and us) to a higher level of thinking when we pray. Don't worry, don't fret, don't fear, don't panic. He says we are to pray in everything. When I don't pray, I'm really saying to God, "I can't trust You with this," or "You can't help me on this one," or "I'm not comfortable giving You control in this area."

Nothing means nothing. Sure, we're not supposed to be anxious about the little things. But Paul even tells us, don't be anxious about legitimate concerns! Don't worry about things you can't change or control. The Lord is near. His Spirit is within you helping you. J. A. Bengel said, "Anxiety and prayer are more opposed to each other than fire and water."[8] Anxiety drains the life out of you. Prayer strengthens you. Billy Graham wrote, "Anxiety is the natural result when our hopes are centered in anything short of God and his will for us."[9] We don't have immunity from fear, anxiety, and stress, but we do have resources that transform our thinking and keep us on track. Paul is not giving cheap advice here; he's offering an alternative. We must know the Word and rest in the Lord.

The only lid on the "everything" is the will of God. All answered prayers are conditioned by His will. My "everything" is bordered by the Word of God—that's my boundary for my praying. Any Scripture I claim is within the will of God. I know myself—sometimes I ask for things I want that have nothing to do with God's will being "done on earth as it is in heaven." The truth is, all I really need is within the will of God. If it's outside the will of God, I don't need it. God cares about little things. The birds of the air. The number of hairs on your head. You can't count all the birds or the hairs on your head . . . but God can. He is in the minute details of life. Paul so wants us to grasp this truth that he just starts piling on words. "Prayer" in the broadest sense is communion with God where you approach Him with your needs. "Supplication" is a sense of need beyond your capacity, a realization of your need for help. "Request" indicates definite and specific prayers.

People worry themselves sick because they don't pray. Worry and anxiety lead to stress and can cause health issues. Instead of worrying, give thanks. Make the choice to rejoice. Here's the formula:

> Be anxious for nothing + Pray about everything = The peace of God will guard your heart

THANKSGIVING

He says we are to pray "with thanksgiving." Paul often ties prayer and thanksgiving together. When I am thankful, I remember all God has done for me in the past. The answered prayers, the unexpected blessings, the healing, the intervention, the resources. Remembering and recognizing what He's done in the past gives me confidence and encouragement for the future. I know that God will hear and will meet me at the point of my need. If He doesn't give me what I want, I know He will give me what I need and that which most glorifies His Son. No matter what is ahead of us as believers, we should always include thanksgiving in our prayers. Be purposeful to pause and thank God for His goodness, grace, and love.

During the winter of 1623 the Pilgrim forefathers were facing desperate and dangerous times. They came to America with hopes of a new life. They were facing a bitter winter without adequate food and supplies. When a ship finally arrived, there were no supplies, only twenty-three additional mouths to feed. It wasn't long before there were more crosses in the cemetery than there were people living inside the stockade. There were seven times as many graves as there were log cabins. They were facing starvation and certain death. Finally, the food ran out. Governor Bradford ordered the storeroom where the corn seed was stored to be opened. This storeroom was their future hope for crops in the spring. He took the corn and rationed five grains of corn to each person per meal. For more than a month they lived on this. Finally, spring came, and they were able to plant, hunt, and fish, and were prepared for the next winter.

It was during that time that the concept of Thanksgiving became a part of the American story—a day we set aside to give thanks for God's abundance and His blessings. But let's go back to that dreadful winter for a moment. When they gathered, they remembered God's provision in the lean times. As they began to settle in and sit at tables filled with food, they would place five grains of corn by each plate to represent God's blessings. It became a tradition that as each person took the grains, one by one, they would say, "I'm thankful for this and this and this and this and this" as they counted their blessings.[10]

THE PEACE OF GOD

How do we learn to rejoice and live in the peace of God? By right praying, right thinking, and right living. We will never learn to think and pray with biblical purpose if we think the goal is happiness or healing. The goal is Jesus. There can be joy in the struggle. Pray with thanksgiving. You may not know why, but God has chosen you to glorify Him in whatever you are going through. Don't waste your sorrows or your suffering. Turn your pain into praise. God has enough confidence in you that He has chosen you to walk through some difficult circumstances. Don't be anxious about your problem or about how God's going to answer. Results are God's problem, not yours. We can rejoice and lay aside our anxieties when we turn our thoughts to God and let Him handle them. Someone once said, "Sometimes God puts His children to bed in the dark."

Joy and peace go hand in hand. These verses are packed with powerful life principles. They only work when they are applied in the crucible of life. These verses aren't theories to be studied but attitudes to be lived out. Gary Miller writes, "Like a three-strand rope, joy, along with peace and prayer, are woven together by those who have come to the end of their own rope. They are not ashamed to admit they have come to the end of themselves, and their own resources. They are relieved to let go, and let God have what they have made. They gently yield to Him to put His handprints all over their lives."[11]

What's the result of being this purposeful in your praying? "The peace of God, which surpasses all comprehension, will guard your hearts and minds in Christ Jesus" (4:7). Your prayers will be returned to you with a peace that you can't explain. It will "guard" your heart. The word there is for a garrison. God will build a fortress of peace around your heart. I'm to take my fears and turn them into prayers. When I begin to pray about everything, I have a growing sense of peace—even when the storm rages. I may not be delivered from the storm, and the circumstances may not change, but I will always have peace.

The peace of God means the hostilities have ended. I am a friend of God and part of His family. I'm not knocking on the door of a stranger; I'm a child of the King, talking to my heavenly Father. The calming impact of the abiding presence of the Spirit is present in my life. When I abide in Him and He abides in me, I don't have to be stressed out. Why? God is not anxious, and I don't have to be either. When I'm faced with a tough situation, I rest in the fact that God is guarding my heart. The enemy is trying to tear down this fortress God has built, but he's not strong enough.

Sometimes I'm impatient with the Lord when it comes to answering prayers. I'm in a hurry and He's not. I want "fast food" answers, and He takes His time. For this all to work, we have to let God guard our hearts and minds. Any wise person will guard who they let into their home. So, believers should guard what we allow to settle in our hearts and minds. Be careful who you let through the door of your heart. Be careful what you let dwell in your mind.

This peace "surpasses all comprehension." I can't get my arms around it. I can't create it or orchestrate it. It's bigger than my abilities to comprehend. I no longer need an explanation. I have a promise from my Father. Peace and comfort don't come through understanding; they come from the Lord. This truth transcends my reasoning abilities. In many ways, God's peace is one of the greatest miracles He performs on the human heart. When circumstances are overwhelming, the peace of God surpasses them. The great miracle of grace is that God can give peace in the midst of the storm. Sometimes we want God to calm the storm, but what He wants to do is calm us in the storm.

If faith is going to be active and operational in our lives, we need to rejoice, let go of our fears, and pray . . . and the peace of God will be the result. But Paul doesn't end there. He moves quickly to how we are to think. You are what you think. It's okay to have an open mind; just be careful what it's open to. Either you rule your mind or your mind will rule you. Erwin Lutzer writes, "The difference between worldliness and godliness is a renewed mind."[12] Paul is clear on what our goals should be. These are purposeful and measurable. We are either growing in these or we aren't.

"Whatever is true . . ." What is true is what God says. Truth is eternal, valid, proven. It doesn't change with climates or cultures. There's a certainty to truth. What is true is the opposite of what is false. Don't buy the lies of the devil and this world's system. Ron Dunn once said, "The things I do know about God enable me to trust Him in areas I don't know about." We should believe our beliefs and doubt our doubts. The things we know about God enable us to trust Him when doubts, fears, and speculations rise up inside.

"Whatever is honorable . . ." That which is worthy of respect, dignified, serious, and reverent. This is a reminder that we should be in awe of our God. He is holy and we aren't. Be careful about laughing at jokes and story lines where God is treated lightly or mocked. This is a matter of being serious-minded.

"Whatever is just . . ." Justice is about what is right or righteous, in right standing with God, in a right relationship with God and others. This is not about what's convenient or popular, but what's right. Make your life decisions about what is right, not what is popular. Knowing what is right to do and not doing it, is a sin (see James 4:17).

"Whatever is pure . . ." This signifies moral purity. The word refers to that which is unmixed or unadulterated. If you have a pure silk tie, there's no polyester in it. Pure means it's not diluted or watered down. My motives should be pure. No mixed motives or hidden agendas.

"Whatever is lovely . . ." That which is acceptable, gracious, and pleasing. Those things that promote harmony and unity. Doing all you can to avoid friction, hostility, and conflict. We are to be peacemakers. We build bridges, not barriers.

"Whatever is commendable . . ." This can have two meanings. It can mean to think on things well spoken of or to think on things we can speak well of. This is the opposite of the Greek word for blasphemy. Don't listen or be influenced by gossips, rumors, or evil speech. Don't embrace a bad report like the people did in the wilderness. If I am dwelling on things that are not commendable, it eventually affects how I think and act toward others. Instead of being a person of prayer, I'll become a walking critic.

"If there is any moral excellence and if there is any praise . . ." This is a catch-all phrase. If I've left something out, this should cover it. The word *excellence* has to do with spiritual excellence. Think on the things that enhance your walk with God and improve your fellowship with God and others. Our God is a God of excellence. Don't settle for being just good enough in your thinking. Excellence should affect all our lives—our worship, our work, and our witness.

When he uses the word *praise*, Paul is referring to anything that gives reason to praise the Lord. Whatever it is, with all of these words, it's about how we think. "Dwell on these things." Ponder them. This is a present imperative in the Greek and means to make it your habit to think this way. Focus on God and not your problems. Do what you know is right, and practice these disciplines daily.

When I live in these truths and renew my mind to the way God wants me to think, then that peace which surpasses every other possible thought will take over. The Philippians had learned and received and heard and seen it in Paul. They knew he wasn't requiring something that was impossible. He had lived this way of thinking and praying before them. His testimony was consistent with his teachings.

Remember, this is a process. It doesn't happen overnight. We have to continually think and do the right things until our new nature becomes second nature. My new mind becomes my daily way of living. When we were teaching my oldest daughter to drive, we practiced in the cemetery so if she lost control she wouldn't kill anybody. When she first started driving, we wouldn't let her play a CD or listen to the radio because we wanted her to focus on driving first. One thing at a time until it's second nature.

All of us are learning to travel life's road. We can be easily distracted or discouraged. If we aren't careful, we'll end up on a detour and lose our way. If we ponder the right things and praise the right way, we will practice the things we have learned, heard, and seen. I want to be remembered for purposeful living, thinking, praying, and dying. Dwell on these things.

CHAPTER 11

PURPOSE BRINGS
CONTENTMENT
Philippians 4:10–23

I am always content with what happens, for
what God chooses is better than what I choose.
—**Epictetus**

The holy person is the only contented man in
the world.
—**William Gurnall**

Be content with what you have, but never with
what you are.
—**W. B. Millard**

IS CHRIST ENOUGH for you? Is He really enough? If all the "stuff" of life were gone, would Jesus be enough? Vance Havner used to say, "It's one thing to say Jesus is all I want, until He is all you have, and then you discover He is all you ever really needed." I must admit, this is an area I wrestle with. Sometimes I get impatient, frustrated, and dissatisfied. I can easily envy what someone else has.

My wife loves to watch HGTV and home renovations or the shows where people are looking for a log cabin in the mountains. I'll sit down to watch a few with her and think, *I wish we had that kitchen . . . that shower . . . that master suite. Man, what I'd give for a closet like that!* Before you know it, I'm dissatisfied with what once made me perfectly happy. I have to ask myself, *Is my purpose to have what I want or to embrace Christ and accept that He gives me what I need?*

People in America seem never to be happy with what they have. We've bought the lies of the advertising industry that convince us we need the latest and greatest technology, a new wardrobe, or that kitchen gadget that will make us an instant top chef. When is enough, enough? I need a little more money. When do you have enough? I need a newer car. But when the payments start and you've financed it for seventy-two months, you wonder if it was worth it. In our church we have people who are very wealthy, and we have people on welfare. I've discovered that money doesn't fix problems; it just buys you a better counselor or medication. If we try to find meaning and contentment apart from Christ, we will be miserable. No matter what you have, there will always be something you don't have.

It is reported that when once asked how much money is enough, tycoon Nelson Rockefeller replied, "Just a little bit more." It seems that contentment often eluded Rockefeller, though he was one of the richest men in the world. King Solomon, likewise, though having amassed all the "success" that money could buy, wrote that it was all vanity—empty, meaningless, unsatisfying. We think that if we get this or have that or marry a certain someone, or drive it, we will be content. But nothing could be further from the truth. The average person, if they don't get what they think they need to be happy, suddenly begins to make irrational decisions. Before long, they change friends, jump churches, switch jobs, and sometimes bail on their marriage. Contentment is a state of the heart, not a state of affairs. It is available to anyone and everyone who is willing to learn its secret.

ARE YOU CONTENT?

There will always be "something else," and we convince ourselves we need it and will go to any extreme to get it. In 1989, the following poem was submitted to "Dear Abby" written by a young man named Jason Lehman. Jason profoundly summarizes our discontent:

It was spring, but it was summer I wanted,
The warm days, and the great outdoors.
It was summer, but it was fall I wanted,
The colorful leaves, and the cool, dry air.
It was fall, but it was winter I wanted,

The beautiful snow, and the joy of the holiday season.
It was winter, but it was spring I wanted,
The warmth, and the blossoming of nature.
I was a child, but it was adulthood I wanted,
The freedom, and the respect.
I was 20, but it was 30 I wanted,
To be mature, and sophisticated.
I was middle-aged, but it was 20 I wanted,
The youth, and the free spirit.
I was retired, but it was middle age I wanted,
The presence of mind, without limitations.
My life was over.
But I never got what I wanted.[1]

The Bible says that Abraham "took his last breath and died at a ripe old age, old and contented" (Gen. 25:8 HCSB). Would people describe our lives in the same way? Will we pass away, satisfied with life? Paul wrote often to the various churches, seeking to help them think properly and maintain an eternal perspective. When he wraps up the letter to the church at Philippi, his parting words are about contentment. Really? This was written by a man in jail, about to be executed. He wasn't writing from a high-rise apartment with a view of the city. His end was near, and things weren't looking particularly sunny, but Paul was content.

> I rejoiced in the Lord greatly once again you
> renewed your care for me. You were, in fact,

concerned about me, but lacked the opportunity to show it. I don't say this out of need, for I have learned to be content in whatever circumstances I am. I know both how to have a little, and I know how to have a lot. In any and all circumstances I have learned the secret of being content—whether well fed or hungry, whether in abundance or in need. I am able to do all things through Him who strengthens me. (Phil. 4:10–13 HCSB)

Paul had learned the secret to life. That word *secret* conjures up all kinds of images and thoughts. I grew up in the 1950s, and my parents loved the TV show *I've Got a Secret* where a celebrity panel had to figure out what the guest did for a living. We have secret societies with secret handshakes and secret rules. Tabloid magazines and gossip media sell stories based on shocking "secrets" they've uncovered. Billions are spent trying to discover secret diets and weight-loss tips. Unfortunately, some Christians are sucked in by preachers who offer "secrets" to power, answered prayer, prosperity, healing, or church growth methods. If it's a secret, why are they trying to sell it? Paul had found the "secret," and he gave it away for free. "I have learned the secret of being content . . ."

The word *contentment* means to be satisfied, or at peace with yourself. It is the opposite of being discontented and dissatisfied. Discontentment will ultimately lead to envy and coveting. Contentment is something we learn; we aren't born with it. It means to be self-contained, to need no outside help or assistance.

In the Greek New Testament the word is also translated "satisfied," "adequate," "competent," or "sufficient." Paul uses the same word in 2 Corinthians 3:5 when he writes that we are not "*competent* in ourselves to consider anything as coming from ourselves, but our competence is from God" (HCSB). The word means "enough" in 2 Corinthians 12:9 when he writes, "My grace is *sufficient* for you." Regardless of the situation, Paul found ultimate, lasting satisfaction in Christ alone.

The original word was used for cities that didn't import things for their people. Why didn't they import goods? They had no need of them; they had enough within their borders. Contentment doesn't say, "I don't care what happens." It is being at peace with Christ's sufficiency. A self-contained city could not be held for ransom. A contented Christian will not sell out. They do not have to go outside of Christ to find what they need.

Over the years, I've had the privilege of visiting the fortress of Masada. Located in the Dead Sea region of Israel, it is on the border between the Judean Desert and the Dead Sea, about fifteen miles from En-Gedi. Masada is a natural fortification, 1,380 feet high on a plateau 1,900 feet long and 1,000 feet wide. The top is flat and is approximately twenty acres. The only two ways up to the fortress were the narrow and difficult climb up the ancient snake path on the eastern side or a path on the western side that was guarded by a tower. In the days of Herod the Great, he turned the mountain of Masada into a fortress, complete with vast cisterns and grain storage areas. He built a luxurious palace there and fortified it to withstand any siege. It is estimated that the twelve cisterns on Masada can hold up to 10.5 million gallons of water. The gardens and storerooms would have sufficiently provided for up to ten thousand men for several years.

The fortress of Masada was "content." It was self-sufficient, no matter what happened. In ancient times, when armies went to war, they would typically try to surround a city and cut off the supply routes. It was a matter of waiting them out until they surrendered. But if the city were a contented city, or a fortress like Masada, such a siege would have possibly taken decades. A contented city had all it needed to go about business as usual despite the outside surroundings.

JESUS IS OUR CONTENTMENT

Jesus is our source and sufficiency. In John 7, Jesus promised an artesian well of supply and sufficiency for all those who come to Him as their source. This is the secret we have to learn. It doesn't happen automatically—it is the result of viewing life from God's perspective. The discontented person is like a thermometer, which registers and reflects the temperature around it. The contented person is like a thermostat, which regulates the atmosphere around it. We tend to be obsessed with our circumstances. They control our emotions and often steal our joy. Paul wants the church to understand that outward circumstances had no effect on him. He was like a thermostat; what he had in Christ couldn't be taken away from him. Everything he needed to live an abundant life was in Christ.

Jeremiah Burroughs was a puritan preacher in England during the seventeenth century. In a book titled *The Rare Jewel of Christian Contentment*, he wrote of the wasted time spent in discontentment. Allow me to summarize his points:

1. It takes away the present comfort of what you have because you do not have something that you want.
2. By all your discontent you cannot help yourselves; you cannot get anything by it.
3. Discontentment and murmuring eat out the good and sweetness of a mercy before it comes.
4. It makes our affliction a great deal worse than otherwise it would be.[2]

Ron Dunn noted, "If your joy depends upon how your kids are doing, you've not learned to be content. It is hard for you to have joy when your teenage son has run off, or when there is rebellion. You let that circumstance rule your life, dominate your every thought. You can't be happy, and you can't experience joy unless everything is perfect in your life. If your joy depends upon the conditions of your job, then you have not learned to be content. Contentment is discovering the sufficiency within yourself so that you have all that you need within yourself."[3] Too often, we put our joy in how we judge the events of our life. The only constant in our life is Christ. He never changes. He is the same yesterday, today, and forever. Others will fail you and let you down. Jesus never fails.

You may say, "God is asking a lot of me. It's too much." He is asking you to allow His character to be formed in you . . .

and He doesn't ask you to do it on your own. He wants you to cooperate with Him as He works in you. Learning contentment is working out what God has worked in me. Charles D. Kelley defines contentment as "the God-given ability to be satisfied with the loving provision of God in any and every situation."[4]

My friend Roger Breland and I often talk about his dad. He was a funny man. Roger remembers as a young man when one of his friends got a car. As Roger talked with his dad about it, his dad said, "He needs it; you don't." Needless to say, Roger didn't get a car. I have friends in the ministry who are never happy. They are always looking for greener grass, comparing salaries, benefit packages, vacation time, and other stuff that really doesn't matter if you are a servant of Christ. If you can't be content where you are, moving certainly won't help you. You'll just take your dissatisfaction with you to your next destination.

Contentment doesn't come by osmosis; it comes by learning and obedience. Paul didn't buy a book or attend a conference about the secret of contentment. He learned it through daily living. In Philippians 4:11 he says, "I have learned to be content." The word for "learned" there is the common word for learning. In verse 12 he says, "I have learned the secret," and the word there is a different word, used by the mystery religions of the day. It meant to be initiated or made aware of a mystery previously unknown. This word implies that learning contentment is a process. Discipleship is a long obedience in the right direction, and so is learning to be content. Paul learned it through difficulties. He gives us a list of the ups and downs of his life, and his was a bumpy road with potholes, land mines, and an occasional place of refreshing. Paul had been from one end to the other and learned that having nothing didn't diminish him and having everything didn't enhance him.

Charles Kelley writes,

> A believer who has learned the skill of contentment has been enabled by God to be satisfied even in the worst conditions. At the same time, however, he can never again be satisfied with the shallow substitutes of contentment that the world has to offer apart from Christ. Once he has tasted Christian contentment he will never again be satisfied with anything less.[5]

Paul, like all of us, had known the highs and lows of life. He had been to the mountaintop and he had been in the pit. Whatever he went through, God was teaching him, molding his life and pruning his heart so that the end result would be contentment.

Too often we judge people by what they have, rather than by who they are. We think, the more they have, the happier they will be. The opposite is often true. The point is, you have Christ and that is enough. Not only is contentment something we learn, but that learning also brings a sense of joy, peace, and satisfaction. It takes away the anxiety about what we don't have and provides a calm assurance and contentment about what we do possess. The world has a viewpoint that says, "What can't be cured must be endured." But Christians can rise above and exclaim, "What can't be cured can be enjoyed!" Paul boasted in 2 Corinthians about his weaknesses, not his strengths.

Can you rejoice and be content if life doesn't go your way? An unplanned pregnancy, an unexpected pink slip, singleness, single parenting, chronic illness, bankruptcy? If we aren't careful, when life turns on us, we will convince ourselves we can't be happy. Elisabeth Elliot suggested, "The answer is not to get rid of unhappiness, but instead to find a new definition for it. Define happiness in things like duty, honor and sacrifice, faithfulness, commitment and service."[6] Earlier in his letter, Paul urged, "What then? Only that in every way, whether in pretense or in truth, Christ is proclaimed; and in this I rejoice" (Phil. 1:18). From beginning to end, Paul reminded them to rejoice. If he could, we should.

Remember, this is a word written by a man who did not have an easy life. If anything, he could have written, "I have learned how to complain." It's not a word you would expect from a man who had been imprisoned, beaten, left for dead, persecuted, shipwrecked, harassed, arrested, criticized, plotted against by the Jews, and beaten severely on multiple occasions.

Paul was at the top of the heap before he came to Christ. He had access to the High Priest, was one of the top dogs among the Pharisees, could have been the next big thing among the Jewish leaders . . . but now he was considered a nobody. His letters are not filled with flowery language from a man immune from problems. He crafted tents to make a living. Paul understood hunger and loss, but whatever the extreme, he had learned the secret of contentment.

If you read further in this chapter, you realize that Paul had led hundreds of people to Christ who had become members of churches he established, but they weren't supporting him in furthering the gospel or helping him when he was in prison. He rejoiced that the Philippians were not in that category. They were givers who demonstrated compassion, sacrifice and joy, all attractive to a lost world that desperately needs all three! Chuck Swindoll writes, "They felt pain when he hurt, they prayed for him when he was unable to stay in touch, and they sent friends to comfort him when he was in prison."[7]

Paul commends them: "For even in Thessalonica [a much wealthier city than Philippi] you sent a gift more than once for my needs. Not that I seek the gift itself, but I seek for the profit which increases to your account" (Phil. 4:16–17). Let's face it, the hardest part of a worship service is getting people excited about the offering. We love to stand, raise our hands, shout for joy, and take notes on the sermon, but when the offering is taken, the church goes quiet. Why? We aren't content, and we are afraid God will ask for some of our stuff and it will take us even longer to be content. The Philippians didn't think that way. I am convinced that how we think about money reveals our level of faith in God's sufficiency. Money and ministry flow together. Our giving reveals our level of spiritual maturity.

> But I have received everything in full and have an abundance; I am amply supplied, having received from Epaphroditus what you have sent, a fragrant aroma, an acceptable sacrifice,

well-pleasing to God. [This was language from the Old Testament to describe an offering that was pleasing to God. Paul was saying, *What you did for me was a sacrifice pleasing to God.*] And my God will supply all your needs according to His riches in glory in Christ Jesus. Now to our God and Father be the glory forever and ever. Amen. (Phil. 4:18–20)

Sometimes our experiences confirm truth, but they are never the final authority. The secret to contentment is knowing that God is running this show and our Father knows what is best. Paul thanked the church for their monetary gift while also reminding them of his contentedness, whether they had sent it or not. Paul didn't need the funds as much as they needed to give them. He remained satisfied, no matter what the circumstances.

AN EDUCATION IN PURPOSEFUL LIVING

If we want to live with purpose, we have to go to a few schools. These schools teach us lessons we must learn in order to live with contentment. In verse 12 Paul tells us he had degrees from the school of humble means and the school of prosperity, the school of starving and the school of feasting. He embraced the truth that nothing is incidental or accidental in the life of the believer. The secret is simple—it's Christ. There's no formula, pill, program, or class to take. It's about embracing Christ as your life.

Paul was content "in whatever circumstances," "in any and every circumstance." He says, "I know how to get along"; "I know how to live." The word there means to abound with more than enough. It's knowing how to adjust to either extreme and be equally content. Paul reminded young Timothy, "But godliness with contentment is a great gain. For we brought nothing into the world, and we can take nothing out. But if we have food and clothing, we will be content with these" (1 Tim. 6:6–8 HCSB).

Major Ian Thomas said the Christian should be a walking miracle. "A miracle is not necessarily something sensational or spectacular. Rather it is something that cannot be explained apart from God."[8] Thomas believed that it is God's intention for us to live in such a way that our lives look miraculous. We are so distinctively different in our thinking, acting, choices, and attitudes that when people observe our lives there is no possible explanation apart from the work of God in our lives.

Have you learned the secret? Paul had. Years ago Don Miller was traveling when his son Gary called and asked where he had eaten that day. Don said, "We ate at a place called Shoney's and they have a sandwich called the Big Boy with a special sauce." Gary told his dad the special sauce was nothing more than Thousand Island dressing. Don insisted it was a special sauce because the restaurant said so.

Paul found the "special sauce," and he had the recipe. It wasn't trying harder or having more stuff; it was having more of Christ and being purposeful in that pursuit. Victor Frankl, in his book *Man's Search for Meaning*, tells the story of spending years in a Nazi prison. He saw firsthand the barbaric acts committed against helpless people. Frankl wrote, "We who lived in concentration camps can remember the men who walked through the huts comforting others, giving away their last pieces of bread. They may have been few in number, but they offer sufficient proof that everything can be taken from a man but one thing: the last of the human freedoms, to choose one's attitude in any given set of circumstances, to choose one's own way."[9]

In another era, Theodore Parker Ferris preached a sermon titled "When Things Don't Go Well." I love the main points of that sermon:

1. Remember that there is nothing that can happen to you that has not happened to millions of others.
2. Remind yourself that as a human being you run the risk of this kind of thing happening.
3. Remember there are people who became great facing what you must now face.
4. Say, "I don't know how I'm going to handle this, but I can. . . . Help that I know nothing about right now will rise up in me, will appear suddenly from all sorts of unexpected places."[10]

When I've made it my purpose to know Christ, and when He makes it His purpose to lead me into an awareness of real contentment, then the promises of God take on a deeper meaning. Paul proclaimed, "I am able to do all things through Him who strengthens me" (Phil. 4:13 HCSB). When you meet some Christians, you might not be sure that verse is in the Bible because they always find a problem, issue, complaint, or something else to be down on.

In his book *To Live Is Christ, To Die Is Gain*, Matt Chandler writes, "Philippians 4:13 is not about chasing your dreams, following your passion, pulling yourself up by your bootstraps, accomplishing anything you want with God's help. . . . It is instead the testimony of those who have Christ and have found Him supremely valuable, joyous and satisfying. . . . Paul found the great constant security, the great centering hope: Jesus Christ Himself."[11]

Greek scholar Kenneth Wuest translated verse 13: "I am strong for all things in the One who constantly infuses strength in me."[12] We are continual recipients of God's strength. Wuest used the word *infuse*, which means to pour, fill, soak, or extract. In the medical field, an infusion is a slow and steady introduction of fluids into a vein. In the spiritual realm, it is God's continual supply of His power into our lives. Contentment is an acknowledgment of dependence. "Apart from Me you can do nothing" (John 15:5).

The Christ-centered life is one that embraces purpose at the highest level, and we have the power to live that life. On a daily basis, in an unending supply, we have all we need. Whatever you face today, Philippians 4:19 is true for you: "And my God will supply all your needs according to His riches in glory in Christ Jesus." Our God meets our needs according to His riches. Faithfulness is recognized by the God who is faithful.

One of the early church fathers was asked how he could be so content. He said, "It consists of nothing more than making a right use of my eyes. In whatever state I am, I first look up to heaven and remember that my principle business here is to get there. Then I look down upon the earth, and call to mind how small a place I occupy in it when I die and am buried. I then look around the world, and observe what multitudes there are who are in many respects more unhappy than myself. Thus I learn where true happiness is placed, where all our cares must end, and what little reason I have to complain."

The sufficiency of Christ drips from verse 19:

- It's personal ("my God").
- It's positive ("will supply").
- It's pointed ("all your needs").
- It's plentiful ("according to His riches").
- It's powerful ("in Christ Jesus").

In Ephesians, Paul talks about the riches of His grace and the riches of His glory. In Romans, he talks about the riches of His goodness and the riches of His wisdom. Out of one of those accounts is an abundance of all you need.

The late George Duncan was a popular preacher from England who wrote a number of books on the deeper Christian life. He once told the story of a man he knew personally who was very wealthy and had one son. The son was a pilot in World War II and was killed in battle. Eventually the old man died, and since there were no heirs to his estate, all he had was sold at auction. An auction house in London was enlisted to handle the affairs, particularly his vast and valuable art collection. On the day of the auction, the auctioneer placed a picture on an easel and opened the bidding. No one had ever seen the picture, a portrait of someone nobody recognized by a painter no one knew. It was, in fact, a portrait of the man's son. No one bid on the picture. The elite in the crowd thought it of no value, though it was actually the key to all the treasures in the estate. In the audience that day was a man who had served the old man for years. He had known the son from the time he was born until the time he died. He bid on the portrait and once he had obtained it, the auctioneer said it was now time for the reading of the will. The will stated that before any of the other artwork could be auctioned off, this simple picture of his son had to be sold. The people present now prepared themselves to bid on what they considered to be the truly valuable pieces. However, the auctioneer closed the auction and said the will further stipulated that whoever got the picture of the son got the estate.

Reverend Duncan once said in a sermon, "Remember, whoever gets Jesus gets the whole lot." The key to contentment is Christ. The key to our purpose is Christ.

ACKNOWLEDGMENTS

No book writes itself. What ends up on the printed page is the result of many people and influences. I'm grateful for those who have helped make this book a reality.

First of all, my wife Terri, who through the years has encouraged me to write. With this book in particular, the truths that men like Ron Dunn, Lehman Strauss, and Vance Havner taught me are in the DNA of every page. Ron in particular taught me to see Philippians in a deeper way.

The members of Sherwood, who listened as I took almost a year to preach through Philippians on Sunday nights. They wanted to go deeper than the typical Sunday morning observer, and I wanted to give them meat not milk. I don't know who got the most out of the messages, me or the church. It was certainly one of my favorite series to preach.

Debbie Toole, who manages my crazy schedule and blocks time for me so I can do what God has called me to do. I couldn't do what I do without her assistance.

Stephanie Bennett, who has painstakingly edited this book. She's moved material around for a better flow, and she knows how I think and write. Her skill set makes me look like a better writer than I really am.

Jim McBride, who is my executive pastor and also my book agent. If Jim didn't handle the day-to-day at Sherwood, I would never have the time to study and write.

To B&H and their incredible staff, for once again believing in me and allowing me to write another book. Bill Craig, Jennifer Lyell, and Taylor Combs have been invaluable in this process. The ReFRESH® series was birthed in a meeting with men who served B&H at the time, while they attended a ReFRESH® Conference. The "Power" series would not exist today if they hadn't given the thumbs up.

NOTES

INTRODUCTION

1. Warren Wiersbe, *Be Decisive: Taking a Stand for the Truth*, OT Commentary—Jeremiah (Colorado Springs, CO: David C. Cook, 2010), 140.
2. John Blanchard, *The Complete Gathered Gold: A Treasury of Quotations for Christians* (Webster, NY: Evangelical Press, 2006), accessed via WORDsearch.
3. Ibid.
4. Martin Manser, *Christian Quotations*, Christian Reference Library Book 2 (2016), Kindle Edition.

CHAPTER 1

1. *The Gospel in Philippians: Displaying God in Godless Times*, Sacra Script Field Notes (Plano, TX: Sacra Script Ministries, 2013), 1.
2. Stuart Briscoe, *Happiness Beyond Our Happenings* (Wheaton, IL: Harold Shaw Publishers, 1993).

CHAPTER 2

1. John Blanchard, *The Complete Gathered Gold: A Treasury of Quotations for Christians* (Webster, NY: Evangelical Press, 2006), accessed via WORDsearch.

2. Ibid.

3. George Duncan, *Sustained by Joy* (London/Glasgow: Pickering & Inglis, 1961), 16.

4. W. E. Vine, *Vine's Complete Expository Dictionary of Old and New Testament Words* (Nashville, TN: Thomas Nelson, 1996).

5. Blanchard, *The Complete Gathered Gold.*

6. Lehman Strauss, *Devotional Studies in Philippians,* 1959, accessed via WORDsearch.

7. William Barclay, *The Daily Study Bible:* First Edition (Biblesoft Formatted Electronic Database Copyright © 2015 by Biblesoft, Inc. All rights reserved.)

8. John Eadie, *A Commentary on the Greek Text of the Epistle of Paul to the Philippians* (BiblioBazaar, 2009), 6.

9. P. Douglas Small, "The Blessings Prayer," © Alive Ministries.

10. John Hull and Tim Elmore, *Pivotol Praying: Connecting with God in Times of Great Need* (Nashville, TN: Thomas Nelson, 2002), 44.

11. E. M. Bounds, *Purpose in Prayer* (New York, NY: Fleming H. Revell, 1920), 96.

12. Author notes from a sermon preached by Dr. Duncan Campbell.

13. Blanchard, *The Complete Gathered Gold.*

14. Ibid.

15. Jeremy Taylor, *The Rules and Exercises of Holy Living,* quoted in *Ronald Dunn, Don't Just Stand There, Pray Something* (Nashville, TN: Thomas Nelson, 1992), 113.

16. Warren Wiersbe, *The Wiersbe Bible Commentary: New Testament* (Colorado Springs, CO: David C. Cook, 2007), 461.

17. S. D. Gordon, *Quiet Talks on Prayer* (New York, NY: Cosimo, 2005), 194.

18. Author notes from a sermon preached by Pastor Ron Dunn at Sherwood.

CHAPTER 3

1. *Shadowlands,* directed by Richard Attenborough, screenplay by William Nicholson (1993; Price Entertainment).

2. Gary Miller, "The Offering," www.garydonmiller.com/blog, January 16, 2014.

3. John Phillips, *Exploring Ephesians and Philippians: An Expository Commentary*, accessed via WORDsearch.

4. This recounting of revival in the nineteenth century is from the following site: https://www.sermoncentral.com/illustrations/sermon-illustration-tom-mccrossan-quotes-prayeradoration-15491.

5. Ibid. From the sermon "Where Do We Go from Here? A Biblical Perspective on the Abortion Battle" by George Robertson.

6. C. H. Spurgeon, *Second Series of Lectures to My Students Being Addresses Delivered to the Students of The Pastors' College, Metropolitan Tabernacle* (London: Passmore and Alabaster, 1877), 163, 171.

7. Tacitus, *Annals* XV. 44.

8. Warren W. Wiersbe, *On Being a Servant of God* (Grand Rapids, MI: Baker Books, 2007), 57.

9. D. Stuart Briscoe, *Bound for Joy*, A Bible Commentary for Laymen (Ventura, CA: Regal Books, 1975).

10. George Duncan, *Sustained by Joy: Studies in Philippians* (London: Pickering & Inglis, 1961), 50.

11. Warren Wiersbe, *The Wiersbe Bible Commentary: New Testament* (Colorado Springs, CO: David C. Cook, 2007), 495.

12. The quotation from Gary Miller was from my notes I took when I heard Miller speak.

CHAPTER 4

1. A. W. Tozer, *God Tells the Man Who Cares* (Camp Hill, PA: WingSpread Publishers, 2010).

2. Shawn Lovejoy, *Be Mean about the Vision: Preserving and Protecting What Matters* (Nashville, TN: Thomas Nelson, 2016), 9–10.

3. Rick Warren, *The Purpose Driven Church* (Grand Rapids, MI: Zondervan, 1995), 103.

4. George Mitchell, *Chained and Cheerful: Paul's Letter to the Philippians* (Scotland, UK: Christian Focus Publications, 2001), 61–62.

5. Gary Miller, "The Choice," garydonmiller.com/blog (January 30, 2014).

6. Ron Dunn, "One Purpose," RonDunn.com, © Lifestyle Ministries.

7. Max Lucado, *It's Not About Me: Rescue from the Life We Thought Would Make Us Happy* (Brentwood, TN: Integrity Publishers, 2004), 8, 73, 92.

8. Gary Keller, *The One Thing* (Austin, TX: Bard Press, 2013), 9–10.

9. Charles Baskerville, *Side-lights on the Epistle to the Philippians* (London: J. Nisbet & Co., 1914), 25.

CHAPTER 5

1. Oswald Chambers, *My Utmost for His Highest*; November 27 devotion online at https://utmost.org/the-secret-of-spiritual-consistency.

2. *Merriam-Webster Dictionary*, "consistent" (accessed online).

3. "The Words of Gardner Taylor," NBC Radio Sermons, 1959–1970.

4. Alexander Maclaren, *Christ in the Heart: and Other Sermons*, accessed via WORDsearch Bible.

5. Vance Havner, *It Is Time*, accessed via WORDsearch Bible.

6. Larry Crabb, *Inside Out* (Colorado Springs, CO: NavPress, 1988), 219.

7. Kenneth S. Wuest, *Wuest's Word Studies from the Greek New Testament*, Volume Two (Grand Rapids, MI: Wm. B. Eerdmans Publishing Co, 1973), accessed via WORDsearch.

8. John Eadie, *A Commentary on the Greek Text of the Epistle of Paul to the Philippians* (New York, NY: Robert Carter & Brothers, 1859), 71.

9. Matt Chandler, *To Live Is Christ, To Die Is Gain* (Colorado Springs, CO: David C. Cook, 2013), 39.

10. Jerry Bridges, *The Practice of Godliness* (Colorado Springs, CO: NavPress, 2008), 181.

11. Ronald Reagan's speech (June 6, 1984) commemorating the Normandy Invasion; https://reaganlibrary.archives.gov/archives/speeches/1984/60684a.htm.

12. Vance Havner, *Why Not Just Be Christians?* (Grand Rapids, MI: Fleming Revell Co, 1964), 35.

13. Francis A. Schaeffer, *The Complete Works of Francis A. Schaeffer, A Christian Worldview, Volume Four: A Christian View of the Church* (Wheaton, IL: Crossway Books, 1985), 189.

14. Vance Havner, *Road to Revival* (Grand Rapids, MI: Fleming H. Revell Company, 1940), 42, accessed via WORDsearch.

15. Ibid., 43.

16. Ibid., 44.

CHAPTER 6

1. James D. Newton, *Uncommon Friends: Life with Thomas Edison, Henry Ford, Harvey Firestone, Alexis Carrel, & Charles Lindbergh* (San Diego: Harcourt, Inc., 1987), 304.

2. William Barclay, *The Letters of James and Peter*, The New Daily Study Bible (Louisville, KY: Westminster John Knox Press, 2003), 345–46.

3. Jon Johnston, *Christian Excellence: Alternative to Success* (Grand Rapids, MI: Baker Book House, 1985), 80.

4. A. J. Motyer, *The Richness of Christ: Studies in the Letter to the Philippians* (London: Inter-Varsity Fellowship, 1966), 65–66.

5. John Blanchard, *The Complete Gathered Gold: A Treasury of Quotations for Christians* (Webster, NY: Evangelical Press, 2006), accessed via WORDsearch.

6. James Moffatt, *The New Testament, a New Translation*, accessed via WORDsearch.

7. This is from Goodspeed online: http://studybible.info/Goodspeed/ Philippians%202.

8. Richard Francis Weymouth, *Weymouth New Testament in Modern Speech*, accessed via WORDsearch.

9. Charles Swindoll, *Improving Your Serve* (Nashville, TN: Word Publishing Group, 1981), 34.

10. C. Gene Wilkes, *Jesus on Leadership: Timeless Wisdom on Servant Leadership* (Carol Stream, IL: Tyndale Publishers, 1998), 13–14.

11. R. C. H. Lenski, *The Interpretation of the Epistle to the Hebrews and The Epistle of James* (Augsburg Publishing House, 1961), accessed via WORDsearch.

12. Adapted from *Lenski's Commentary on the New Testament*, Hebrews 12.

13. Gayle D. Erwin, *The Jesus Style* (Palm Springs, CA: Ronald N. Haynes Publishers, 1983), 18–20.

CHAPTER 7

1. Quote by Alistair Begg, http://gracequotes.org/quote/moralism-says-to-unbelievers-be-what-you-are-not-christianity-says-to-believers-be-what-you-are.

2. Lehman Strauss, *Devotional Studies in Philippians*, 1959, accessed via WORDsearch.

3. Guy King, *Joy Way: An Exposition of the Epistle of Paul to the Philippians* (Pennsylvania: Chistian Literature Crusade, 1952).

4. Strauss, *Devotional Studies in Philippians*.

5. John Blanchard, *The Complete Gathered Gold: A Treasure of Quotations for Christians* (Webster, NY: Evangelical Press, 2006), accessed via WORDSearch.

6. F. B. Meyer, *Meyer's Devotional Commentary on Philippians;* see https://www.studylight.org/commentaries/dcp/philippians-3.html.

7. Vance Havner, *Pepper 'n' Salt,* accessed via WORDsearch.

8. Sam Gordon, *An Odyssey of Joy: The Message of Philippians* (Ambassador-Emerald International, 2004), accessed via Logos Bible Software.

9. Joseph W. Stowell, *Simply Jesus and You* (Colorado Springs: Multnomah, 2006), 16.

CHAPTER 8

1. A personal email sent to me by Tom Elliff.

2. The journals of Jim Elliot, October 28, 1949, http://www2.wheaton. edu/bgc/archives/faq/20.htm.

3. Charles R. Swindoll, *Laugh Again* (Nashville: Thomas Nelson, 1992), 134.

4. J. H. Jowett, *The High Calling* (New York: Revell, 1909), 131.

5. Paul S. Rees, *The Adequate Man* (New York: Revell Publishing, 1959), 70.

6. Hannah Whithall Smith, *The Christian's Secret of a Happy Life* (New York: Revell, 1952), 32.

7. Richard Francis Weymouth, *Weymouth New Testament in Modern Speech,* accessed via WORDsearch.

8. Ernest R. Campbell, *A Commentary of Philippians and Titus based on the Greek New Testament* (Silverton, OR: Canyonview Press, 1990).

9. A. W. Tozer, *The Knowledge of the Holy* (New York: HarperCollins, 1961), 64.

10. Mark Batterson, *All In* (Grand Rapids, MI: Zondervan, 2013), 13–14.

11. Ron Dunn, *Faith Crisis* (Nashville: B&H, 2013), 221.

12. T. C Stallings, *Playing on God's Team* (Racine, WI: BroadStreet Publishing Group, 2017), 64.

13. Tony Dungy, *Uncommon: Finding Your Path to Significance* (Carol Stream, IL: Tyndale, 2011), 24.

14. Ibid., 154.

CHAPTER 9

1. The Gospel in Philippians, SacraScript.org.

2. J. B. Lightfoot, *St. Paul's Epistle to the Philippians* (London: Macmillan and Co., 1873), 142.

3. Richard Francis Weymouth, *Weymouth New Testament in Modern Speech*, accessed via WORDsearch.

4. Vance Havner, *Pepper 'n' Salt* (New York: Revell, 1966), accessed via WORDsearch.

5. Ibid.

6. J. A. Motyer, *Jesus Our Joy: The Message of Philippians* (InterVarsity Press, 1984).

7. Lehman Strauss, *Devotional Studies in Philippians*, 1959, accessed via WORDsearch.

8. Havner, *Pepper 'n' Salt*, 83.

9. *Life Application Bible Commentary – Philippians, Colossians, & Philemon*, accessed via WordSearch.

CHAPTER 10

1. Gary Miller, "The Devotion," www.garydonmiller.com/blog, March 15, 2016.

2. Karen Mains, *The Key to a Loving Heart* (Elgin, Ill: David C. Cook, 1979), 143–44.

3. Marshall Shelley, *Well-Intentioned Dragons* (Minneapolis, MN: Bethany House, 1994), 11.

4. George M. Stulac, *The IVP New Testament Commentary Series – James*, 1993. Accessed via WordSearch.

5. Anonymous quote used by C. H. Spurgeon in *My Sermon-Notes: A Selection from Outlines of Discourses Delivered at the Metropolitan Tabernacle* (New York: Funk & Wagnalls, 1888), 192.

6. Warren W. Wiersbe, *The Bible Exposition Commentary: Old Testament, Wisdom and Poetry (Job – Song of Solomon)* (Colorado Springs: David C. Cook, 2004), 165.

7. John Blanchard, *The Complete Gathered Gold: A Treasury of Quotations for Christians* (Evangelical Press, 2006), accessed via WORDsearch.

8. Ibid.

9. Ibid.

10. See https://www.thenewamerican.com/culture/history/item/4737-five-grains-of-pilgrim-corn.

11. Gary Miller, "The Peace," www.garydonmiller.com/blog, February 22, 2014.

12. Blanchard, *The Complete Gathered Gold*.

CHAPTER 11

1. Jason Lehman, "Present Tense," letter to Dear Abby in the *Chicago Tribune*, February 14, 1989.

2. Jeremiah Burroughs, *The Rare Jewel of Christian Contentment* (London: L. Sadler and R. Beaumont, 1651).

3. Ron Dunn, "Secret of Contentment," RonDunn.com, © Lifestyle Ministries.

4. Charles D. Kelley, "The Miracle of Contentment," *Discipleship Journal*, no. 42 (1987), 29.

5. Ibid., 31.

6. Elisabeth Elliot quoted in *A Thankful Heart in a World of Hurt* by Joni Eareckson Tada (Rose Publishing: 2015), 12.

7. Chuck Swindoll, *Laugh Again Hope Again: Two Books to Inspire a Joy-Filled Life* (Nashville, TN: Thomas Nelson, 2009), 205.

8. Charles D. Kelley, "The Miracle of Contentment," *Discipleship Journal*, no. 42 (1987), accessed via WORDsearch.

9. Viktor Frankl, *Man's Search for Meaning* (1959; Boston, MA: Beacon Press, 2006), 65–66.

10. Maxie D. Dunnam, *The Preacher's Commentary: Galatians, Ephesians, Philippians, Colossians, Philemon* (Nashville: Thomas Nelson, 1982).

11. Matt Chandler and Jared C. Wilson, *To Live Is Christ, To Die Is Gain* (Colorado Springs, CO: David C. Cook, 2013), 200.

12. Kenneth S. Wuest, *The New Testament: An Expanded Translation* (Wm. B. Eerdmans Publishing Co, 1961), accessed via WORDsearch.

ALSO AVAILABLE FROM MICHAEL CATT

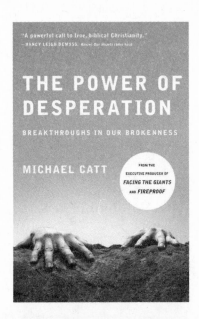

"A powerful call to true, biblical Christianity."
—NANCY LEIGH DEMOSS, *Revive Our Hearts* radio host

THE POWER OF DESPERATION

BREAKTHROUGHS IN OUR BROKENNESS

MICHAEL CATT

FROM THE EXECUTIVE PRODUCER OF *FACING THE GIANTS* AND *FIREPROOF*

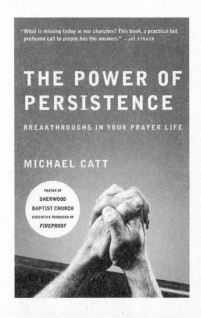

"What is missing today in our churches? This book, a practical but profound call to prayer, has the answers." —JAY STRACK

THE POWER OF PERSISTENCE

BREAKTHROUGHS IN YOUR PRAYER LIFE

MICHAEL CATT

PASTOR OF SHERWOOD BAPTIST CHURCH EXECUTIVE PRODUCER OF *FIREPROOF*

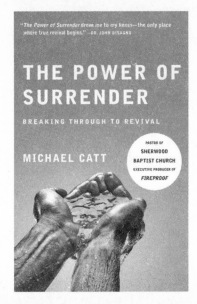

"*The Power of Surrender* drove me to my knees—the only place where true revival begins." —DR. JOHN BISAGNO

THE POWER OF SURRENDER

BREAKING THROUGH TO REVIVAL

MICHAEL CATT

PASTOR OF SHERWOOD BAPTIST CHURCH EXECUTIVE PRODUCER OF *FIREPROOF*

"You will be captivated by these pages . . . and drawn into a fresh relationship with the One who gives us our purpose in life!"
—JAMES T. DRAPER JR., *President Emeritus, LifeWay Christian Resources*

THE POWER OF PURPOSE

BREAKING THROUGH TO INTENTIONAL LIVING

MICHAEL CATT

PASTOR OF SHERWOOD BAPTIST CHURCH EXECUTIVE PRODUCER OF *FIREPROOF*